ONE WEEK LOAN

Realising Benefits from Government ICT Investment

- A fool's errand?

by

Stephen Jenner

Copyright ©Stephen Jenner 2009
First published 2009
Academic Publishing International Ltd, Reading, UK
info@academic-publishing.org

Second Printing February 2009
Third Printing June 2009

ISBN: 978-1-906638-26-9

Outside cover image courtesy of Jonathan Zander

Printed in Great Britain by the MPG Books Group, Bodmin and King's Lynn

Dedication

For Peter

Contents

List of examples and figures

Preface

The genesis for this book came from three sources – firstly an increasing concern that whilst we accept the reason we invest in programmes is to deliver business benefits, the reality is that many organisations struggle to demonstrate the realisation of those benefits in practice. This problem is compounded by the fact that it's clearly not a new framework that we need (there are already many value measuring frameworks in existence – some of which are described in this book) rather there is something more fundamental that needs addressing. I should also stress that whilst the focus here is on ICT and IT enabled business change, the issues, principles and techniques discussed are of general applicability.

The second stimulus came from John Suffolk, UK Government CIO, who suggested that I should capture the lessons learned from developing and applying a benefits management regime to the Criminal Justice System IT portfolio. This approach was recognised internationally and won the 2007 Civil Service award for Financial Management. Whilst this book includes the key features of that approach, it however goes beyond it and represents the conclusions of personal experience over more years than I care to remember, lessons from a wide variety of environments and research undertaken into what works in relation to benefits realisation.

The third driver for this book was the feedback received from attendees at workshops, seminars and conferences in the UK, North America, Europe and Australia. This feedback, both at the time and in subsequent correspondence, highlighted that there is a widespread recognition that our current approaches are flawed and that the solution lies in a radically different approach that encompasses the techniques outlined in this book.

This book is therefore ultimately the result of personal experience, research and a series of conversations between myself, colleagues, practitioners and academics as I have sought to resolve the benefits paradox outlined above. I hope this book will assist you in redressing the balance, but the debate continues – please feel free to e-mail me with your comments, observations and suggestions.

Stephen.jenner5@btinternet.com

Foreword by John Suffolk, UK Government CIO

Demonstrating a positive return from our investments in technology enabled business change, in financial or enhanced performance terms, has never been more important. The current climate of increasing financial constraint means that potential investments come under increased scrutiny, and consequently, if we are unable to articulate the value of IT, then potentially value-creating projects may be put at risk. Additionally, a focus on cost reduction rather than value creation, can lead organisations to decisions that fail to adequately exploit the capabilities and capacity created by previous investments. Being able to demonstrate the value from IT is therefore crucial to organisational health - as a basis for prioritising investment decisions, to demonstrate effective corporate governance, and most significantly, as a basis for managing the creation of value on an active, on-going basis. This is a challenge that faces the public and private sectors alike.

The good news is that some organisations in both sectors have adopted 'best of breed' practices that confound the assumption that benefits realised necessarily fall below those forecast. In this book Stephen Jenner has captured these learnings from both practical experience and academic research. The result is an approach to benefits management that is radically different from the one that we too often encounter in practice. As such it's an approach that focuses on value throughout the project life cycle, which is based on ensuring the investment justification is robust, and which manages benefits from an enterprise rather than a project basis. Most importantly it is an approach that has been shown to work in practice. The application of many of the techniques outlined will need to be adapted to the particular circumstances of each organisation, but the principles that Steve outlines are of general applicability. I commend them to you.

John Suffolk, UK Government Chief Information Officer

Foreword by Frank Bannister, Trinity College Dublin

Governments were amongst the first to make large scale investments in computing. Indeed, in the early years of computing, governments were often at the leading edge in the application of the latest technologies. Today, notwithstanding the extensive use of outsourcing, the modern state, in its various manifestations, remains one of the largest single buyers of information and communications technology (ICT).

It would be comforting to be able to say that all of this money has been well spent. Alas, the history of government computing is dotted with what, in the worst case can only be described as computer disasters, and in the best as poor investments. It is probably true to say that governments are neither better nor worse than the private sector in managing and in extracting value from ICT. Unfortunately for the public sector its computer failures tend to be just that – public. Equally embarrassing private sector failures are often quietly buried, far from the shareholders' gaze.

Given this, it is not surprising that managing public sector ICT projects to ensure not only that they deliver value, but are seen to deliver value, continues to be a pressing concern of government. Furthermore, while benefits management and ICT evaluation are both complicated and challenging at the best of times, where project objectives include transformational change, they are doubly so. In an era where transformational government has become de rigeur, the publication of this book is, therefore, especially timely. Stephen Jenner brings to this work many years of expertise, experience and achievement in ensuring that major public sector ICT systems projects deliver value. This is a book that should be mandatory reading not only for all public sector CIOs, but for any manager who is responsible for investing in or managing major ICT systems.

Frank Bannister, Trinity College Dublin

Acknowledgements

The techniques, tools and concepts discussed in this book have been shaped by discussion and debate with numerous professional colleagues and practitioners from across the globe, and by the contributions of attendees at over 30 workshops and benefits management seminars over the last two years. In particular, I thank the following professional colleagues for their insight, commitment and humour: Mark Browning, Jon Chadwick, Donna Dalton, Karen Farquharson, Manjit Jaswal, Rajan Khakhar, Lisa Stewart, and Nick Walker.

I'm deeply indebted to Professor Bent Flyvbjerg at Aalborg University, whose extensive research provided confirmation of my increasing conviction, based on practical experience, that too often business cases constitute a form of 'benefits fraud'. Leading academics in the field of realising benefits from ICT who have influenced my thinking include: Professor Donald Marchand at IMD, Professor Dan Remenyi at Henley, and Dr Frank Bannister at Trinity College Dublin. Their contributions can be seen throughout this book.

Others who have helped provide my thinking with a more rounded perspective include Matthew Snaith, Susan Goldsworthy and Mike Davies, and I thank them for their support, advice and encouragement.

I should also pay tribute to my benefits team who developed and applied the principles outlined here to the CJS IT portfolio between 2005 and 2008, and in particular: Jennifer Wallace, Jonathan Fearon, Jill Thibaut, Monica Hiew, Stuart Bromwich, Rob Davis, Gareth Bell, Christopher Munday, Tim Laken, Rachel Kenehan and Kirsten Mitchinson. They are the real heroes of this story

Introduction

So what's the problem?

Despite a plethora of books on benefits management, advice from consultants, academic research and the development of numerous frameworks to capture the value of investments in IT and IT-enabled change over the last 20 years, we are still struggling to demonstrate and derive the full potential value from that investment – and this applies in both public and private sectors, for example:

- Benko and McFarlan (2003) report that in the United States, "*a staggering 40% of information technology (IT) investments fail to deliver their intended return each year.*" But that should hardly come as a surprise when, "*A recent study reveals that 80% of IT projects are conceived of and funded in a fragmented manner, with little in the way of overall planning.*" In the public sector, a report from Booz Allen Hamilton (2002) stated, "*A recent assessment in the President's Management Agenda contends that the $45 billion investment in IT during FY01 has not produced measurable gains.*";

- In the UK, Ward and Daniel (2006) note that, "*The statistic that over 70% of IT projects are seen to fail to deliver the intended benefits is well known, both among members of the business community and the IT community itself.*" In relation to the public sector, the Public Accounts Committee commented in 1999 that, "*for more than two decades, implementing IT systems successfully has proved difficult ... implementation of IT systems has resulted in delay, confusion and inconvenience to the citizen and, in many cases, poor value for money to the taxpayer.*";

- In Europe, a report in 2006 on the results of investment in e Government initiatives, concluded that, "*After at least a decade of large investments (running into billions of Euro) at digitalizing the public sector, governments in Europe are still mostly unable to objectively quantify and show the benefits and returns of such investments.*"; and

- In Australia, Sohal and Ng (1998) found that the potential of IS/IT had not been fully utilised in business due to inadequate and inappropriate appraisal and evaluation of proposed projects, and a report for the OECD in 2006 noted that, "*Data from Aus-*

tralia on achieved benefit/cost ratios [in] central government indicates that rates of return on ICT investments often are low or negative."

As we shall see in Chapter 1, research highlights that this is a widespread and continuing issue affecting both public and private sectors. The position may be even worse since, as we shall see, many business cases lack a consistent and quantified statement of the anticipated benefits and many organisations fail to assess the realisation of benefits from their investments in projects and programmes. There is also evidence that the benefits used to justify investments are often exaggerated to an extent that verges on 'benefits fraud'.

Why is this important? Well, firstly, if we don't know the value to be derived from our investments, we can't make best use of the funds at our disposal – the 'good' lose out to the 'bad' but well presented proposals; secondly, if we don't know where the value is we cannot manage it; and thirdly, it's taxpayers' and shareholders' money, and it is therefore incumbent upon those making investments that they are able to demonstrate a sound investment justification and a commitment to realising all potential forms of value.

A new framework is not the answer – according to Andresen et al there were at least 30 IS/IT investment evaluation methodologies in 2000, and this number has increased since then with value measuring methodologies being developed in the US and Australia as we see in Chapter 5. But if a new framework is not the answer, what is? Or is demonstrating value from ICT projects 'a fool's errand'?

I argue the answer is 'yes', but not in the usual sense of the term, as I explain in Chapter 1. The solution lies in a different mindset, based on an approach that manages value on an active basis, which is derived from empirical research and practical experience, and which combines three key elements:

1. Planning effectively for benefits realisation by ensuring the benefits claimed in business cases are robust and realisable. This is the subject of Section 1 of this book.

2. Identifying and capturing all forms of value created. This is introduced in Chapter 3 and then is covered in detail in Section 2.

3. Realising the benefits, and going beyond benefits realisation to value creation. This is explored in Section 3.

In its application, this is a radically different approach to the one that we most commonly see failing in practice, but it is one that has been proven to work in a variety of environments. As such it is built on the following key principles:

- Benefits management starts with the business case – experience and research demonstrate that failing projects rarely have brilliant business cases. Ward and Taylor (1996) argue, *"It has often been observed when analysing IS/IT project failures that all the ingredients for failure existed on Day One of the project, or even before it started!"* So start with the business case and ensure it is developed with the end in mind i.e. conditions change and the business case needs to adjust to reflect these changes, but throughout it all we need to be *'clear about the benefits we are buying'.* In short, what impacts on organisational costs and performance are we investing in ICT to achieve? The business case should in effect be a value case where the focus is on the benefits, rather than delivery of a solution. We are buying benefits not kit!

- Following on from the above, benefits are the raison d'etre of investments, costs are a constraint. Benefits should therefore be managed as, if not more, robustly as project costs.

- Optimism bias and strategic misrepresentation (see Chapter 1) are an empirical reality and benefits claimed are often little more than unsubstantiated assumptions masquerading as facts – we therefore need a Benefits Eligibility Framework and periodic integrity checks to ensure benefits are robust and realisable. Most significantly, benefits should be agreed with the recipients and those who will be responsible for realising them <u>prior to investment</u>.

- Capture all forms of value created – efficiency (both time and financial savings), effectiveness (improved performance), the foundation or potential opportunity value inherent in infrastructure investments and, particularly in the public sector, wider social and political value – and apply these categories from business case preparation, through investment appraisal and portfolio prioritisation, to benefits realisation. This is important because if you are not concerned with capturing value you can hardly be committed to value creation, and if you're not concerned with creating value then you shouldn't be entrusted with somebody else's resources – and as Larry 'the Liquidator' Garfield said in the film of the same name, it's "*other people's money*".

- 'Book' the benefits wherever possible – in departmental head-counts, efficiency plans and performance targets, but also check that the benefits are realised, and that for example, savings are not achieved at the expense of output and service quality.

- Plan and manage benefits realisation on an organisational or enterprise rather than a project basis – with a forward-looking focus directed at learning and planning for success rather than on attributing blame. Be pessimistic in planning but optimistic in implementation. Use benefits measures that tap into what is important to the user, and continually ask, "*is that the best we can do?*"

- Go beyond planned benefits to exploit learnings and leverage capabilities and create value by engaging the IT function, project teams and the business users in a continuous exploration of, "*what might be*".

It should be noted that the three key elements of Active Value Management outlined above – ensuring all benefits forecasts are robust and realisable, capturing all value created, and realising the full potential benefits from our investment in ICT, are interdependent and mutually supportive. Rather than being sequential stages, they represent an iterative process in which one lays the basis for the others. But it is usually good advice to start at the beginning, so we commence by considering how we can ensure our benefits forecasts are robust and realisable.

Section 1
Ensuring benefits claimed are robust and realisable

"Trust everyone, but cut the deck"

PT Barnum

After reading this Section you will:

Understand why a robust approach to benefits planning is a pre-requisite for effective benefits management and what can go wrong when one is absent. In particular you will understand the prevalence of optimism bias and its more insidious bedfellow, strategic misrepresentation.

Recognise the three key building blocks of a comprehensive and effective benefits planning framework:

- a consistent benefits classification methodology utilising a bi-dimensional benefits grid;
- a 'benefits eligibility framework' that determines what benefits can be counted, how they are quantified and valued; and
- a benefits planning process, including validation of benefits claimed, that lays the basis for benefits realisation.

Be in a position to design and implement an effective benefits planning process to guide more informed investment appraisal and portfolio selection decisions, and maximise the probability that forecast benefits will be realised in practice.

The objectives of Benefits Planning are threefold.

Firstly, to ensure all benefits claimed are robust and realisable so that the organisation can select the portfolio of ICT projects, programmes and initiatives that represent an optimum return on the available investment funds. This return can be in terms of cost savings, increased revenue, strategic contribution, legal or regulatory compliance and supporting business as usual. This is the focus of this Section of the book.

Secondly, to provide a basis for capturing all value created. This is important because as we say in the Introduction, if we are not concerned with capturing value, we can hardly be interested in creating value. We consider some generic approaches to capturing value in relation to efficiency and effectiveness benefits in this Section. We then consider the more specialist areas of cross-departmental projects, social and citizen value, mandatory and infrastructure projects in Section 2.

Thirdly, benefits planning lays the basis for benefits realisation in practice which is considered in Section 3 – experience demonstrates conclusively that without the disciplines outlined in Chapters 2 and 3, organisations will continue to fail to generate the returns forecast by their portfolio of ICT projects and programmes and performance will continue to fall short of the promise.

For the time being though we focus on effective benefits planning. We start in Chapter 1 by considering what we mean by 'benefits' and 'benefits management'. We then review the evidence that indicates that benefits forecasts are rarely as reliable as we would like to think and what solutions can be adopted to resolve this issue.

This leads on to consideration in Chapter 2 of how we can establish a consistent benefits classification methodology utilising a bi-dimensional benefits grid. This is important because it enables 'level playing field' comparisons between projects and against actual performance over time – and so provides a basis for meaningful accountability. We then go further to consider guidance on which benefits should be counted, how they should be quantified and valued – in short, a 'Benefits Eligibility Framework'.

We then turn in Chapter 3 to consider how all the above can be brought together in a benefits planning process that lays the basis for benefits realisation in practice

Chapter 1
Benefits, Benefits Management and Reliable Forecasting

"Trust in God but tether your camel."

Sufi parable

Introduction

Our starting point is a recognition that the reason organisations invest in projects and programmes, including ICT, is to realise benefits.

> *"The fundamental reason for beginning a programme is to realise benefits through change. The change may be to do things differently, to do different things, or to do things that will influence others to change."*
>
> Office of Government Commerce (2003)

and

> *"what the business really cares about is not systems, but benefits"*
>
> Gartner (2005)

But what do we mean by 'benefits' and what exactly is 'benefits management'? The OGC (2003) defines benefits as, "*The quantifiable and measurable improvement resulting from an outcome which is perceived as positive by a stakeholder and which will normally have a tangible value expressed in monetary or resource terms. Benefits are expected when a change is conceived. Benefits are realised as a result of activities undertaken to effect the change.*"

Other definitions cover similar ground, for example:

> *"A benefit is an outcome of change which is perceived as positive by a stakeholder...Usually benefits are of value to the organisation and measurable."*
>
> Bradley (2006)

> *"Benefits are real sources of value to the business, such as increased revenues, better customer retention, lower costs or quicker time-to-market".*
>
> Gartner (2005)

> *"A term used to indicate an advantage, profit or gain attained by an individual or organization."*
>
> Remenyi, Bannister and Money (2007)

7

The key points to note from these definitions are that benefits can be:

- Tangible or Intangible. Tangible benefits are those which are relatively easy to measure, whilst intangible benefits refer to those that are not so easy to measure reliably. The latter may include benefits such as improved staff morale and decision-making, although in most cases proxy indicators of such benefits can be developed (I use the term indicator to emphasise that the link with the benefit is less certain than with measures).

- Direct or Enabled. Direct benefits are those that are directly realised as a result of a project or programme. In contrast, enabled benefits refer to those where realisation of the benefit is dependent on business change to exploit the capability the investment has created. The majority of ICT benefits are enabled i.e. they are only realised when the investment in technology is combined with business process re-engineering and people change, including training and re-deploying staff to other value-adding activity.

- Financial or Economic. Benefits can have a direct monetary value in terms of costs saved and/or revenue generated (financial benefits) or can be the monetary value attributed to some performance improvement (economic benefits). The OGC's 'Managing Successful Programmes' states that, "*Ideally, benefits should be quantified and measured in monetary terms.*" This reflects the guidance in the HM Treasury Green Book that, "*The general rule is that benefits should be valued unless it is clearly not practicable to do so*" and, "*The NPV is the primary criterion for deciding whether government action can be justified.*" It is however crucial that we distinguish between benefits which are financial in nature (for example, cost savings and revenue generated) and those where the monetary figure represents the estimated economic value assigned to the underlying benefit, such as some improvement in organisational performance, quality of service or reduction in risk of systems failure. This distinction is of fundamental importance because the benefit that we are buying is the performance or quality improvement or reduction in risk, not some arbitrary monetary value assigned as part of the Net Present Value calculation. Representing such investments as having a positive return on investment can be misleading as it confuses financial return with attributed economic value, and this can divert attention from actually managing those investments so that value is created. More on this in due course.

Seen from an organisational or enterprise perspective, most end benefits fall into one of the following categories reflecting the four fundamental generic investment objectives of projects and programmes:

- *Investment Objective 1: Revenue generation* – where the benefit is increased revenue from greater sales.

- *Investment Objective 2: Cost savings/efficiency* – where the benefit is reduced costs or the ability to respond to increased demand within the limits of current resourcing, so reducing unit costs.

- *Investment Objective 3: To support an organisational strategy or business priority* – benefits in this case relate to the contribution made to a business strategy. They are often enabling in nature and are linked in a chain of cause and effect from the project to the business strategy (see Chapter 3).

- *Investment Objective 4: Because you have to* - i.e. the project or programme is in response to a legal or regulatory requirement, or to maintain business as usual. In such cases the benefit is compliance with those requirements and therefore avoidance of the costs (financial or otherwise) associated with non-compliance or systems failure. More on this in Chapter 6.

Most fundamentally, a benefit is something that is of value to someone – and this value can vary from stakeholder to stakeholder. Value is a relative not an absolute concept – as Molière said, "*Things only have the value that we give them.*" It is consequently a fundamental principle of effective benefits management that the value of a benefit should be determined by the recipient. A project may claim to deliver a benefit of 10% or £10,000, but if the business won't sign up to deliver that benefit it is unlikely that it will be realised. We will re-visit this issue throughout the book.

We should also distinguish between the terms 'benefits' and 'value' – we use these terms to some extent interchangeably to emphasise the point that benefits are not an economist's or accountant's technical term, but rather refer to some improvement that is of value to the organisation, its staff or its customers/clients. But it is also helpful to distinguish between the two terms – we see benefits as the specific individual improvements arising from an investment in ICT, whereas value is a more generic and collective term comprising all benefits realised from an investment.

9

So if that's what benefits are, what do we mean by 'Benefits Management'? The key point to note is that benefits are usually dependent on change and this requires <u>active</u> management. In other words projects can be completed to schedule and budget, but the benefits are usually only realised when some change in working practices occurs i.e. when we combine investments in ICT systems with business process changes and 'people' changes – ranging from training to use the system, to re-skilling and redeploying staff to other value-adding activities.

The OGC (2005) states that the aims of Benefits Management are, "*to make sure that desired business change or policy outcomes have been clearly defined, are measurable, and provide a compelling case for investment – and ultimately to ensure that the change or policy outcomes are actually achieved.*"

The OGC's 'Managing Successful Programmes' goes further in identifying seven objectives of benefits management:

1. ensure benefits are identified and defined clearly, and linked to strategic outcomes;
2. ensure business areas are committed to the identified benefits and their realisation, to encourage ownership and responsibility for 'adding value' through the realisation process;
3. proactively manage the process of benefit realisation, including benefits measurement;
4. keep benefits within realistic boundaries of scope and value, to identify their wider impact;
5. use the benefits to direct the programme and provide a focus for delivering change, to realise benefits in line with overall business direction and strategy;
6. ensure benefits realisation is tracked and recorded, and ensure achievements are properly identified and recognised; and
7. provide alignment and clear links between the programme, its vision and desired outcomes, and the strategic objectives of the organisation(s) involved.

Benefits Management is therefore a process that runs throughout the project life cycle – from investment justification and preparation of the business case, through project implementation, and beyond project closure to business as usual. It is a process that encompasses benefits identification, forecasting, validation, tracking/reporting and harvesting or realising benefits. It has three main objectives. Firstly, it seeks to ensure that investment decisions are made on the basis of a robust and clear understanding of the potential benefits – in short, there should be no confusion about what benefits are being bought. This is addressed Chapters 2 and 3. Secondly, benefits management concerns capturing all forms of value created – to ensure our investment decisions are value led and to lay the basis for benefits realisation. This is addressed in Chapters 3-7. The third element concerns ensuring that forecast benefits are realised and that we go beyond this to capture benefits as they emerge and create value by exploiting capability and capacity on an on-going basis – this is addressed in Section 3.

So far so good, but the whole process depends on reliable data – so that we select the 'right' projects, know what benefits are expected from an investment and, in due course, so that we know whether they are being realised. Unfortunately, both personal experience and empirical research shows that benefits data is rarely as reliable as we would wish.

Benefits reliability

When it comes to appraising and evaluating benefits we face an immediate problem, namely the absence of an agreed set of rules by which benefits are classified, quantified and valued. This is in stark contrast to the other side of the 'value for money' coin, costs, where a plethora of guidance exists in the form of:

- Financial reporting rules such as Financial Reporting Standards, International Accounting Standards and Generally Accepted Accounting Practice (GAAP);
- Management accounting best practice – for example, as promulgated by the Chartered Institute of Management Accountants (CIMA) and any of the multitude of Management Accounting text books; and
- Organisations' own guidance contained in finance manuals, policies and procedures.

With benefits in contrast, there is little definitive guidance provided to determine what benefits should be included in business and investment cases and how to value them. This is a significant gap because, as the UK Treasury Green Book says, "*There is a demonstrated, systemic tendency for project appraisers to be overly optimistic. This is a worldwide phenomenon that affects both the private and public sectors...appraisers tend to overstate benefits*".

The situation is further complicated because there is often no agreed benchmark against which benefits are assessed and consequently the scale of such benefits' 'optimism bias' is not known with any certainty.

Indeed a study for HM Treasury by consultants Mott MacDonald (2002) found an average benefits shortfall of only 2% - but there were two problems with this. Firstly, some business cases didn't give any indication of the forecast benefits and without this one cannot reliably assess the scale of forecasting error or optimism bias. Secondly, most did not have any post implementation review to confirm the scale of benefits realisation and consequently determining achievement of benefits was based on personal interpretation. The result was that, according to the researchers, they were unable to provide an estimate of benefits forecasting error due to the absence of reliable data!

Other studies have found evidence that forecasts are systematically overstated. Most notably, research by Flyvbjerg et al (2005) of 210 road and rail projects across 14 countries on five continents, valued at US $59bn (2004 prices) found, "*very high statistical significance that forecasters generally do a poor job of estimating the demand for transport infrastructure projects*". This was particularly true for rail projects with an average 106% overestimation and, estimates that were, "*highly, systematically, and significantly misleading (inflated). The result is large benefit shortfalls.*" The problems were also found to extend to road projects where around half had more than +/-20% estimation error (measured against the Full Business Case). Furthermore, the research also found that forecasts have not become more accurate over the 30 years studied. These results mirrored those found by the same researchers in 2002 in relation to cost estimates. The results are significant - Flyvbjerg quotes Bangkok's Skytrain where passenger forecasts were 2.5 times more than actual. The result was that the system was over-provisioned with platforms longer than required, idle trains and an obvious impact on operating costs. Other famous (infamous) examples include the Dome in London, where visitor numbers were overestimated by between five and six million depending upon whether you include the 1 million free tickets given to school children reported by the BBC.

So what we see is a tendency for benefits forecasts to be overstated – and this extends beyond the large public sector infrastructure projects that are commonly the subject of empirical research. The OGC's Successful Delivery Toolkit (2005) reported, for example, that, "*30-40% of systems to support business change deliver no benefits whatsoever*" (despite them presumably having been approved on a cost benefit basis under the mandatory HM Treasury Green Book rules) and KPMG's Global IT Project Management Survey 2005 found that, "*project success appears to equate to achieving an acceptable level of failure or minimizing lost benefits*".

It can be argued that this may result from a legitimate source i.e. that we are dealing with an uncertain future and consequently, the results of any initiative are subject to estimation error. This is of course true, but the research referred to above found that future uncertainty can not explain the scale and consistency of results found – if this was the cause we would expect to see: a more balanced picture of over and under-estimating of benefits; an improvement over time as more sophisticated forecasting methodologies have been developed and employed; and greater accuracy as forecasters adapt their estimates to reflect their real world experiences. Kahneman and Lovallo (2003) however note that even experts appear to fail to learn the lessons of previous experience, or if they do, they do not apply this learning well to their own estimates and forecasts resulting in what psychologists refer to as the planning fallacy or, "*The tendency to hold a confident belief that one's own project will proceed as planned, even while knowing that the vast majority of similar projects have run late*".

Cognitive biases are clearly part of the explanation for optimism bias. Tversky and Kahneman (1979) demonstrated that people, including experts, are prone to making errors in estimating such as being overly optimistic about outcomes and our ability to control them, are unreasonably risk averse and surprisingly poor at estimating probabilities (more on this in Chapter 6). People also tend to attribute success to their skills, dedication or intelligence, but to blame external factors for failure. The consequence is that forecasters suffer from what Lovallo and Kahneman (2003) refer to as, "*delusional optimism...They overestimate benefits and underestimate costs. They spin scenarios of success while overlooking the potential for mistakes and miscalculations.*"

But there is also evidence of a less legitimate cause of benefits over-estimation – that business case writers and project sponsors know in advance that the benefits claimed will not be realised, but they claim them anyway to get the funding required, confident that they won't be held to account for their non-realisation. Gartner (2005) quotes one IT practitioner as saying, "*We do go through the business case benefit process and look at the discounted cash flow, payback period and ROI. It is, however, very seldom that business sponsors are held accountable for delivering project benefits*". Ward (2006) reports that the results of an international survey of Benefits Management practices found, "*over 90% state the main purpose of the business case is to secure the project budget. However, 70% believe they are failing to identify and quantify the benefits adequately and 38% openly admit they often overstate the benefits in order to obtain funding.*" In another study Peppard et al (2006) comment that, "*the traditional investment appraisal process is seen as a ritual that must be overcome before any project can begin, with many benefits be-ing overstated in order to get projects through the appraisal process."* Australian researchers Lin et al (2005) report that, *"in 26.2% of cases, the respondents openly admitted that their current processes actually overstated the benefits in order to get approval."* The fact that professionals admit to over-estimating benefits (see also Wachs, 1989) suggests the issue may be even more prevalent than surveys suggest. Indeed, these findings are reflected in the conclusions of Flyvbjerg et al (2005) who argue that the scale of forecasting error found by their research can only be explained by a factor they call, *"strategic misrepresentation"* or in the colloquial, *"lying"* – in the sense that those presenting the business case know that the benefits are over-stated (and costs under-stated) and the purpose of so-doing is to persuade (or one might argue, to deceive) the funding bodies into making an investment that they might otherwise not have so done.

The desire to present a case for funding in as favourable a light as possible is understandable, but problems occur when the argument is made irrespective of the facts. Too often making a positive case, slips over into practices that at best constitute being 'economical with the truth' or which are, to paraphrase Alan Clark, *"economical with the actualité"*. These practices include:

- *Double Counting* ('what's yours is mine') – this occurs when projects are inter-dependent and one claims the benefits of another or even worse, both claim each other's benefits, The result is that the same benefits can be claimed by more than one project and at a portfolio level, costs may even exceed the benefits that will be realised in total. In one portfolio over 60% of the claimed benefits were found to be double counted.

- *Spurious claims and over-estimation of impact* – because benefits are not validated in advance and there is no effective accountability for their realisation, there is little incentive for business case writers to ensure that the benefits claimed are capable of realisation. In one case, benefits were originally forecast at £55m per annum. After deployment when it came to certifying the benefits actually realised, the business was only willing to commit to a revised total of £300k over 10 years. The issue was compounded by the fact that it was in no one's interests to drive up the benefits since that was perceived as only inviting further budget cuts.

- *Ignoring the impact of other projects and 'heads in the sand' benefits reporting* - more than one project can claim an impact on a target without taking into consideration the reduction in potential impact as the quick wins and 'low hanging fruit' disappear. In practice, benefits realisation is rarely linear and diminishing returns set in. Seen individually such claims may appear justifiable, but when seen in their entirety they are less tenable – for example, when five projects separately claim a 10% impact that may be reasonable on an individual basis, but there is little chance of a combined 50% impact overall as the marginal cost of process improvement increases.

- *Inconsistent valuation* – this is a particular issue where staff time savings are concerned as inconsistent valuation can result from differing approaches to costing productive time and overheads. In one programme the value of an hour saved for a member of staff being paid £30,000 pa varied from £15 in one department, to over £33 in another, due to differing assumptions about how much productive time is worked in a day and how many productive days there are in a year. The scope for inconsistency increases further when one takes into account differing approaches to whether indirect costs and overheads can be included in the 'efficiency savings' forecast. This is usually uncovered when benefits are valued at 'fully loaded' rates at the time of the Business Case request (to help produce a positive NPV) but subsequently only the marginal value at best is realised.

- The, *"You're the beneficiary ('whether you know it or not')"* scenario – this concerns cases where benefits are forecast to be received by another department or agency but are not actually validated with that body. In one example, a project business case forecast that benefits of £24m pa would be delivered to another organisation, but these benefits were not agreed in advance with anyone who could, or more importantly would, be held to account for their realisation. As a result after deployment the booked benefits did not cover the running costs let alone the sunk costs of design and development.

- *Phantom benefits* – these include opportunity value or non-cashable efficiency benefits where there is no indication as to how they will be realised or what the time saved will be used for. In one major programme costing over £250m, benefits of in excess of £70m a year were forecast from greater efficiency and time savings that would enable staff to be re-deployed from administrative to more value-adding activities. In the event, when it came to reporting on benefits realisation, it became clear that this claim represented the potential that could be realised if management was able to re-deploy parts of staff (the time saved rarely equated to a whole person). This also highlights the importance of the point made above about not confusing financial with economic benefits – the value here was not a cash saving but time savings. A greater focus at an earlier point on how such time savings would be realised would have paid real dividends. Other examples of phantom benefits include instances of notional costs avoided that are correctly included in the options appraisal stage, being claimed after the investment decision (this is discussed further under cost avoidance benefits in the next Chapter) and when a project claims a benefit that appears to be logical but there is no underlying substance, rationale or logical analysis to support the claim made. Strategic Contribution Analysis, Benefits Maps and Root Cause Models discussed in Chapter 3 can help identify and validate such benefits.

- Pay now, benefit later (a long, long time later – or at least after those responsible are a long time gone and no longer liable to be held to account for realisation) – this is a particular issue with projects and programmes with long payback periods. It also emphasises the importance of adopting phased or modular approaches to system development, where benefits are delivered even if the whole programme is never delivered, and managing benefits from an organisational rather than project perspective. These issues are addressed in Chapter 9.

- *The 'centre of the universe' syndrome* – this is an extension of the double counting issue referred to above, where projects claim to enable everything along the lines of, "*you couldn't use the PC without the table, so the table claims the benefits of the PC.*" This may seem ridiculous but it is not as rare as we would like to think.

So what empirical research and personal experience have identified is a form of 'benefits fraud': business cases are presented for funding where those making the case are at best negligent and at worst complicit in a form of deception – deception because they know the benefits presented to justify the investment are unlikely to ever be realised in sufficient scale to justify the investment of taxpayers' or shareholders' funds. This is important because as Flyvbjerg et al (2005) say, it results in, "*A make-believe world of misrepresentation that makes it extremely difficult to decide which projects deserve funding and which do not."* The result is according to Flyvbjerg, in a presentation at the University of California, *"the survival of the unfittest"* where projects are funded when they shouldn't be and consequently others don't get funding when they should, *"had they not lost out to projects with "better" misrepresentation."* (Flyvbjerg et al, 2002).

Whether the cause is delusion, due to the cognitive biases referred to above, and/or to deception, the solution clearly lies beyond a set of rules for classifying and quantifying benefits – for one thing, the forecasting errors found with regard to benefits have also been found in relation to costs (see the Mott MacDonald and Flyvbjerg et al (2002) studies referred to above) where the absence of rules can hardly be used to explain the scale of estimating 'error'. Consequently we need to look more widely at a range of solutions that encompass:

- Subjecting investment proposals to independent review, scrutiny and challenge. Ayers (2007) has suggested that boards should have an *"'Advocatus Diaboli'…whose job it is to poke holes in pet projects. These professional "No" men could be an antidote to overconfidence bias."* A Value Management Office (see Chapter 9) can also play a useful role here in challenging the assumptions that underpin benefits forecasts and asking are they reasonable? I pose the question, is demonstrating a return on ICT a 'fool's errand'? The answer from this perspective is 'yes' – in the sense of the court jester whose role included telling the monarch things that no one else would dare to say, and who was consequently, as Feste in Twelfth Night, *"wise enough to play the fool."*

- Ensuring benefits are validated with the recipients prior to investment and booking them wherever possible in efficiency plans, budgets, performance and headcount targets, and individuals' performance agreements (see Chapters 3 and 8).

- Evidence-based forecasting using past experience from similar projects to inform benefits forecasts or what is termed 'reference class forecasting' (see Chapter 3) to overcome the planning fallacy and organisational pressures to overestimate benefits.

- Accountability mechanisms that hold people to account for results, by tracking performance through to benefits realisation (see Chapter 8) – if business case writers and project sponsors know that they will be held to account for their promises, then there is more of an incentive for them to ensure these promises are realistic.

- Governance based on 'planning for success' rather than attributing blame i.e. an active forward-focused search for learnings and applying these learnings to future investments. This also needs to be supported by a shift in the organisational dynamics away from misrepresentation and optimism bias, in favour of robust and realisable forecasts, based on a clear understanding about expected standards of behaviour (see Chapter 9).

But whilst a set of benefits rules are only part of the answer, they do underpin the effectiveness of the other factors mentioned above – by providing a consistent and robust framework against which to assess benefits claims, track performance, and a common language in which business and IT professionals can engage in a meaningful on-going dialogue about how to create value from the investment in ICT. It is to this set of benefits rules, the Benefits Eligibility Framework, that we now turn.

Chapter 2
The Benefits Eligibility Framework

"Without an acquaintance with the rules of propriety, it is impossible for the character to be established."

Confucius

Introduction

We saw in the previous chapter that optimism bias and strategic misrepresentation are an empirical reality. An agreed Benefits Eligibility Framework that ensures benefits forecasts are robust and realisable, and which lays the basis for benefits realisation in practice, is therefore an absolute prerequisite for effective benefits management. As such it consists of two key elements:

1. a consistent benefits classification system that reviews benefits from more than one perspective using a Benefits Grid; and
2. a set of rules that determines what benefits can be counted, how they are valued and how they should be validated.

We consider each key element in turn.

Benefits Eligibility Framework 1 – A Benefits Classification system

A common classification system enables us to categorise benefits on a consistent basis and this in turn facilitates: business case preparation; investment appraisals and portfolio prioritisation; and tracking benefits from forecast through to realisation.

But what classification system should we use? Experience indicates the factors that need to be considered in selecting an appropriate benefits classification system include:

- *Complete/Fully inclusive* – the system should be flexible enough to accommodate all relevant benefits;
- *Mutually exclusive/Unambiguous* – the categories used should be sufficiently different as to minimise confusion as to what category individual benefits best fit;
- *Wide applicability* – the classification should operate at project, programme and portfolio level, facilitating comparisons between investments and over time;
- *Simple* – the categorisation used should be easy to understand; and

- *Self checking* - ideally, the system should support the validation of claimed benefits and help deter and detect double counting.

The categorisation of benefits suggested by the OGC in 'Managing Successful Programmes' is as follows:

- Direct financial – benefits that are realised by the programme and can be measured in monetary terms.
- Direct non-financial - benefits that are realised by the programme but which are not financial in nature.
- Indirect benefits – those that result from the direct benefits or from changes enabled by the programme.

The HM Treasury Green Book suggests a similar analysis between:

- Financial quantitative – such as operating cost reductions and increased revenue.
- Non-financial quantitative – such as fewer customer complaints.
- Non-financial qualitative – such as improved staff morale.
- Outcomes – which can be both quantitative and qualitative such as improved health care and public safety.

The approach proposed by Ward and Daniel (2006) represents a further development in that it incorporates consideration of benefits from two perspectives – they argue that benefits are derived from changes that enable organisations to do new things, do things better or stop doing things; and they also classify benefits into categories based on degree of 'explicitness' as: financial, quantifiable, measurable and observable. These two perspectives can then be combined in a grid. The advantage of such an approach is that it recognises the multi-dimensional nature of benefits and that not all benefits can be claimed or demonstrated with the same degree of confidence – we explore the issue of confidence assessments further in Chapter 3.

The advantages of a bi-dimensional approach are also recognised in an approach that has been found to have significant advantages in a major change portfolio context where benefits crossed organisational boundaries. This approach examines benefits from two perspectives – analysis by benefits type and analysis by recipient. The results can be presented in a benefits grid - see Figure 1.

Benefit Recipient	Benefit Type			
	Efficiency		Effectiveness	
	Cashable	Opportunity Value	Cashable	Opportunity Value
Organisation/ Department 1				
Organisation/ Department 2				
Organisation/ Department 3				
Organisation/ Department 4				
Totals				

Figure 1: The Benefits Grid: Benefits categorisation by type and recipient

Perspective 1 - Benefits analysis by type

First, benefits are categorised as efficiency or effectiveness and are then sub-divided into cashable and opportunity value (non-cashable) categories. Many organisations will have their own definitions of what constitutes 'cashable' (and in some ways what really matters is not whether such benefits are cashable but whether they are cashed in practice – more on this later) but the following definitions have been found to work well in practice:

Efficiency Benefits – including staff time, equipment and other cost savings. These benefits are realised in: reductions in operating budgets; increased output for the same input cost (with consequently lower unit costs); and in time savings which can be re-deployed to other value-adding activities or which enable existing activities to be completed to a higher standard of quality.

Effectiveness/Strategic Benefits – these are benefits that contribute to a strategic target or business priority. When expressed in monetary terms, such benefits are described as 'effectiveness' benefits (but note that this is an economic rather than financial value, to emphasise that the value won't be realised in monetary form – more on this below).

Efficiency and effectiveness benefits are then sub-divided into Cashable and Opportunity Value categories.

Cashable Benefits: There are four types of benefit that can potentially be classified under this heading:

1. Current output is maintained but at lower input cost so that budgets can be reduced. Such benefits are financial in nature.
2. Additional output or throughput is achieved but for the same input cost i.e. budgets are unaltered but unit costs fall. These benefits can be measured in terms of the increased throughput or output, or in financial terms i.e. the value of the reduction in unit costs.
3. Improving the quality of current activity or output with consequent financial savings elsewhere in the system.
4. Increased productivity that enables savings to be achieved elsewhere – for example, staff time savings can allow staff to take on extra tasks that would otherwise have required the recruitment of additional staff or overtime working. The crucial point here is that additional cost is avoided – if not, the benefit is an opportunity value, see below. As in the second category above, these benefits can be measured in terms of the additional activity undertaken or in financial terms, as the costs avoided from not having to employ new staff or the overtime no longer required.

Opportunity Value: This refers to instances where staff time is saved but there is no consequent financial saving in budgets, unit costs or costs avoided. Instead the staff time is re-deployed, either deliberately or non-deliberately, on activities that would otherwise not have been undertaken. The result may be (or may not be as we shall see) an improvement in quality, outputs and outcomes. The point to note is that the time saving may be realised in improved efficiency or effectiveness benefit terms depending on what use is made of the time saved.

Perspective 2 - Benefits analysis by recipient

This is important for four reasons. Firstly, it is a reality of the early years of the 21st century that business and government are increasingly joined, or joining up. As a consequence, the benefits from many IT and IT-enabled business change projects and programmes will cross departmental and organisational boundaries. This diversity in benefit recipient needs to be reflected in our classification framework. Secondly, it helps address the problems of forecasting error and optimism bias discussed above, by requiring the recipient of the benefit to agree to realise the benefits prior to investment – the recipient is usually less prone to over-estimating benefits since they will be required to realise them in due course. Thirdly the probability of benefits realisation is increased when benefits are agreed with the recipients since they will often be required to deliver the business change on which benefits realisation is dependent. Early consultation on benefits also helps operational managers prepare for the business changes that will be required to realise the benefits. Lastly, it helps address the ever-present issue of double counting – whilst more than one project may claim a benefit, agreement with the recipients helps identify double counting because they will usually only agree to realise it once.

So, a benefits classification system provides the foundation for effective Benefits Management by helping ensure benefits claimed are robust and by laying the basis for their realisation. But on its own it's not enough - it needs to be enhanced by a set of rules about how benefits will be quantified, validated and valued. When the classification system is combined with such rules it constitutes a Benefits Eligibility Framework.

Benefits Eligibility Framework 2 – A common rule set

As highlighted above, the absence of a common set of rules concerning the quantification, validation and valuation of benefits compromises effective investment appraisal, portfolio management and benefits realisation because there's no level playing field against which to appraise potential investments and against which to track benefits across the ICT project portfolio through to realisation. There is consequently a need to codify the rules that an organisation chooses to live by in managing the benefits from its portfolio of projects and programmes. When these rules are brought together in a single place they constitute a Benefits Eligibility Framework that builds on the benefits classification system to provide:

1. a set of rules about what benefits can and can't be claimed, how they should be valued and what validation methodology is to be used in appraising and prioritising business cases for investment;
2. a consistent approach across the organisation's portfolio providing a level playing field against which to compare projects and programmes;
3. a methodologically sound approach to measuring and valuing benefits realisation; and
4. a basis for making meaningful comparisons over time.

The framework should apply to all projects and programmes included within the portfolio and from investment appraisal and funding decisions, through benefits realisation reporting to post implementation evaluation reviews. But, besides a description of the benefits classification system, what else does a Benefits Eligibility Framework need to include? At a minimum it needs to address the following key areas:

- Guidance on identification and quantification of benefits
- Benefits validation
- Benefits valuation
- Benefits tracking and measurement
- Treatment of cost avoidance benefits
- Intangibles
- Disbenefits
- Miscellaneous issues including addressing the risk of double counting.

Guidance on identifying, quantifying and validating benefits is addressed in the next chapter, whilst tracking and measurement is considered in Chapter 8. We therefore leave these aside for the time being and focus on the issues of benefits valuation, cost avoidance benefits, intangibles, disbenefits and addressing double counting.

Benefits valuation

Key principles covered under this heading are: the need to avoid confusing financial and economic benefits; valuing benefits at marginal cost unless there is clear evidence that overheads will be reduced; and focusing on the use to which staff time savings are put.

Some organisations require all benefits to be expressed in monetary terms to support investment appraisals based on discounted cash flow techniques. This includes central government in the UK, where the Treasury Green Book requires all benefits to be valued wherever feasible and Net Present Value is the preferred decision criterion. As noted already, there is a risk that managers will confuse the attributed monetary value with the real nature of the benefit - we consequently need to distinguish between financial benefits and those that may have a monetary (or economic) value attributed to them, but where the underlying benefit relates to time savings or some performance improvement, rather than an increased cash inflow or reduced cash outflow. It is therefore recommended that where monetary values are attributed to non-financial benefits, they are referred to as economic benefits to distinguish them from financial (cashable) benefits.

Whilst cashable benefits are relatively straight-forward to value, the valuation of time savings and performance improvements is more problematic with plenty of scope for "benefits padding". Where available, the organisation's standard costings should be applied with clarity over the treatment of overheads. It is strongly recommended that a key valuation principle should be to value staff time savings on a marginal cost basis for benefits realisation purposes unless there is evidence and confidence that savings in fixed overhead costs (accommodation, light and heating etc) will also be realised – for example by closing an office. Having said that, it is also important that records are kept of the cumulative effects of the portfolio on staff time savings - a project may only save an hour or so of each person's time a week, but when this is combined with other projects, there may well be greater scope for redeploying staff and realising savings in overhead costs. This role can be performed by the Value Management Office as discussed in Chapter 9.

It is common practice to value time savings at the marginal cost of labour particularly in the public sector. The Treasury Green Book for example, states that time savings should be valued at, "*the opportunity cost of the time to the employer. This will be equal at the margin to the cost of labour to the employer: the gross wage rate plus non-wage labour costs such as national insurance, pensions and other costs that vary with hours worked.*" Yet it should not be forgotten that unless staff time savings are 'cashed' in terms of reduced budgets or lower unit costs, the value of the time saved is not the marginal cost of labour, but the value of the activities undertaken in the time saved. The Benefits Realisation Plan (see the next Chapter) should identify how this potential value will be realised.

In the public sector, valuing benefits to citizens, and indeed to wider society, is a specialist area and is covered in depth in Chapter 5.

Cost avoidance benefits

It is absolutely right that business cases should take into consideration the costs associated with not taking action, but the subsequent treatment of costs avoided as part of the benefits management regime will depend on the nature of these costs. Costs avoided can come in a multitude of forms and treatment will depend on the circumstances, for example:

- The running costs of existing legacy systems replaced by a new system – such costs avoided should either be re-cycled to help fund the new system (so appearing as a reduction in the costs required rather than as a benefit) or alternatively they should be realised by extracting them from the operating budgets (as cashable efficiency savings).

- Improved service reliability resulting in less system outages or downtime. Such benefits are not really cost but time savings (see the example below) and consequently the focus should be on deciding how the time saved will be used.

- Uncertain future costs associated with the failure of legacy systems – unless provision for such costs is already built into operating budgets, benefits realisation can not be tracked in any meaningful sense. Such potential benefits may be included in the options appraisal but are no longer relevant once the decision to invest is taken. See the case study below.

- The benefits of choosing one project option over another in achieving a given policy objective – for example, where an IT system to meet a policy objective costs £1m compared with £1.5m for a manual system. These notional costs avoided (i.e. £0.5m in this example) are relevant in the options appraisal, but the notional incremental costs associated with pursuing the next best option/alternative are, as above, not relevant once the investment decision has been made. They should therefore not be included in the benefits management regime.

Perhaps more than any other, this area is one in which organisations need to pay particularly close attention to ensure that they understand the true nature of the benefits claimed and whether they will be realised in any meaningful sense. It is also crucially important that we distinguish between direct and enabling benefits on the one hand, and on the other, those benefits that are considered as part of the options appraisal, but which cease to be relevant once a particular option is selected i.e. from a benefits management perspective the only benefits we are concerned with are those that are relevant to, and are derived from, the preferred option. This is highlighted by the example below.

Example 1 – Cost avoidance benefits
The following example illustrates the importance of validating claims of cost avoidance and, more fundamentally, understanding the true nature, and hence value, of different types of cost avoided.

Background
An organisation was considering the cost avoidance benefits associated with the failure of legacy systems in their business case for a replacement IT system. Two types of benefit were identified:

1.1   Unrecoverable failures arising from factors such as unavailability

---

of hardware to replace failing equipment and lack of capability to support the software. In the event of such a failure, and in the absence of an alternative IT system, the organisation would need to revert to paper based manual systems to operate business critical processes. This was valued on the basis of the cost of the estimated additional administrative staff required to operate the manual processes. Estimates were then adjusted for the probability of failure over the forecast life of the new system with the assigned probability rising in year 1 from 0.15 to 0.5 by year 5.

1.2 Recoverable failures. Replacement of the current system would also reduce the amount of system downtime. Based on an analysis of downtime over the previous six months, and the number of users at each site, estimates based on the value of staff time saved were calculated.

Appraisal
It is right that the business case should consider the costs of not acting and consequently cost avoidance should be taken into consideration in the appraisal of whether to invest in a replacement system, but the analysis required further work to provide an assurance that the figures claimed represented a fair and accurate representation of the most likely value of uncertain future events. In particular:

In relation to the value claimed from avoiding an unrecoverable systems failure, confirmation:

- from operational management that the additional administrative staff forecast as being required to operate manual processes was a fair estimate; and
- that the cost of those staff was the marginal gross salary cost;
- some justification for the rather arbitrary probabilities assigned to systems failure each year.

In relation to the value attributed to recoverable failure of the legacy system:

- assurance from operational management that the estimates of down time were reasonable and that the hourly rate used was the marginal salary cost; and
- the impact on operational staff of down time i.e. that lost time was actually that – or putting it the other way, if the system didn't go down management would gain additional staff time.

This second bullet point above highlights the fact that unless management were planning to reduce headcount, the value of the time saved from avoiding down time was not the marginal cost of labour, but the activities those members of staff could engage in. Consequently the key questions were what would management do to realise these time savings, what value would they have and how would management assess whether they had been realised or not?

The point to stress is that the bulk of the 'costs avoided' were not costs avoided at all – they represented time savings that were available for value adding activities.

Intangibles

Programmes often aim to deliver or enable some form of organisational culture change with business cases referring to intangible or soft benefits such as improved morale and more collaborative/joined-up working. Treatment of such benefits will vary from organisation to organisation and the Benefits Eligibility Framework should provide clear guidance as to how such benefits should be treated. The scale and extent to which such benefits need to be managed in practice will depend on their relative importance to the organisation and the ease of measurement, but just because a benefit is difficult to measure does not mean that the attempt should not be made to quantify and, if possible, to value it – indeed if a benefit can't be measured it really should not be used to justify the investment. A report to the US National Electronic Commerce Coordinating Council in 2005 for example, concluded that, "*Justifications for projects usually include a long, predictable list of "intangible benefits". The problem here is that there is no such thing; all benefits are realised in terms of costs, revenue, or significant political gain. To call a benefit "intangible" simply means that nobody has been able – or has done enough analysis – to develop a quantifiable measure.*" The paper goes on to cite the example of "*user friendliness*" where training costs and error rates should be lower, whilst productivity should be higher.

As to valuing such benefits, the Treasury Green Book advises, "*In the absence of an existing robust (i.e. reliable and accurate) monetary valuation of an impact, a decision must be made whether to commission a study...Where it is concluded that a research project to determine valuations is not appropriate, a central estimate together with a maximum and minimum plausible valuation, should be included.*" The Green Book (and the supplementary guidance: 'Managing Risks to the Public: Appraisal Guidance') also contains guidance on valuing non-market impacts such as a prevented fatality, with contingent valuation techniques that are discussed further in Chapter 5.

HM Treasury guidance (2005) also recognises that, "*there may well be advantages and disadvantages that cannot be expressed in monetary terms... If they are important to consider, they should still be clearly described. Such advantages and disadvantages may well be crucial to the decision in an appraisal.*" Guidance from the OGC (2003) concurs - "*Even if monetary quantification is not possible, all benefits should be quantified numerically.*"

As outlined above, it is rare that a benefit cannot be measured in some way – using proxy indicators if necessary. For example, improvements in staff morale can be measured via staff satisfaction surveys, absenteeism levels, staff turnover rates and exit surveys. Similarly, sophisticated approaches to measuring customer satisfaction based on an analysis of the drivers of customer satisfaction are possible (see Chapter 5).

Disbenefits

Disbenefits are defined by the OGC (2003) as, "*the negative impacts of change.*" In principle, all costs required to realise the benefits claimed should be reflected in the Business Case. Where these costs escalate or unforeseen costs are incurred, such costs can be treated in two ways:

- by increasing the cost shown in the business case and in project funding requests. This will be most relevant where the additional costs fall on the project or its sponsoring organisation; or

- by treating these additional costs as a disbenefit. This approach will be particularly relevant where the additional costs fall on an organisation separate from the one delivering the project. These 'disbenefits' should be included in the project business case updates and benefits realisation reports so that management attention is directed at mitigating the effects wherever possible.

Miscellaneous issues

Besides the above (and the areas of quantification, validation and tracking that are considered in Chapters 3 and 8) the Benefits Eligibility Framework should also address issues such as:

- Shared benefits - the Benefits Eligibility Framework can help address double counting by providing guidance on treating benefits to which more than one project contributes, for example:

29

- By treating such projects as part of a larger programme with the combined cost/benefit position being disclosed;
- Agreeing to split the benefits between the projects on an equitable basis such as agreed contribution or on the basis of relative size of total applicable costs;
- Project business cases reporting two Net Present Values – one based on the benefits delivered directly by that project; and the other including all the benefits (and costs) from the wider programme to which they contribute.

- Double counting (or indeed triple counting) of benefits is a particular problem in organisations with a large portfolio of projects and programmes, and particularly where these projects and programmes cross organisational boundaries. Addressing this issue requires validation of benefits with the recipient wherever possible – unless they are incompetent, recipients will be unlikely to sign up to realising the same benefit more than once. Other checks include comparing benefits across the project portfolio to identify areas where benefits may appear reasonable at an individual project level, but are less so when the accumulated position across the portfolio as a whole is examined. This is another role that can be undertaken by a Value Management Office as discussed in Chapter 9.

- The period over which benefits can be claimed - normally the assumed useful lifetime of the assets.

- Amendments to the framework - it needs to be a 'living' document, and should therefore be subject to regular review and approval by the relevant governance body.

The Benefits Eligibility Framework provides a sound basis for ensuring that benefits are robust and realisable and as such it provides the context for Benefits Planning. It is to this that we now turn.

Chapter 3
Planning for Benefits Realisation

"In preparing for battle I have always found that plans are useless,
but planning is indispensable."

Dwight D. Eisenhower

Introduction

So far our journey has identified the scale of error often encountered in benefits (and cost) forecasting. The Benefits Eligibility Framework, and classification system, were introduced and they lay the basis for ensuring benefits are robust by providing a comprehensive and consistent basis on which to compare projects and track benefits through to realisation. So far so good, but we also need to consider how we identify or 'capture' benefits. As already explained, most benefits are not automatically realised. Realisation depends on reallocating resources, re-engineering of business processes and training users on using and how to exploit the capacity and capability created. Consequently if we don't plan for the realisation of all potential benefits, value usually just drifts away. We therefore need to consider how to:

1. Identify, quantify and value all potential benefits. In this chapter we focus on some generic techniques for identifying and quantifying potential benefits. This sets the scene for more detailed consideration in the next Section of how we can capture and value the benefits from cross-organisational, mandatory and infrastructure projects and programmes, as well as in the public sector, benefits to citizens and wider society.
2. Validate benefits i.e. how we ensure that the benefits identified above are robust and realisable. We examine general approaches to benefits validation as well as specific considerations relating to validating efficiency and strategic benefits.
3. Summarize the above in Benefits Profiles and a Benefits Realisation Plan, which provides a basis for tracking benefits through to realisation.

These three stages in benefits realisation planning are considered in turn.

Stage 1 - Identifying and quantifying benefits

A potentially powerful technique for identifying both efficiency and effectiveness benefits is Benefits Mapping or Modelling, and this is enhanced when it is combined with practitioner workshops. This in turn provides a basis for quantifying (and in due course, valuing) the scale of the benefits identified.

Benefits Mapping comes in a variety of forms but what is common to them all is an attempt to understand the cause and effect, or the "if, then", chain by which benefits will be realised from investment in ICT projects and programmes. These methodologies include:

Benefits Modelling. The approach recommended by the OGC's '*Managing Successful Programmes*' maps: enablers (ICT and business changes), intermediate benefits, and end benefits. These categories are linked in a cause and effect chain - for example, web-based customer information (the enabler) may result in fewer queries (an intermediate benefit) and this in turn can reduce organisational spend (the end benefit). There is an important point here – business cases can on occasions list dozens of benefits, but the focus should ultimately be on the end benefits and the contribution of the initiative to the generic investment objectives identified in Chapter 1: saving money, generating revenue, contributing to a strategic target or business priority, maintaining business as usual, or meeting a legal or regulatory requirement.

Root Cause Modelling which seeks to articulate the logic underpinning claims of project impacts on the root causes of major systemic issues. A detailed example is provided in Chapter 4.

Benefits Dependency Networks (BDNs) as suggested by Cranfield University's Information Systems Research Centre (Ward and Daniel (2006)). This approach was derived from the Precedence Diagramming Method and maps:

- Left to right - the business and enabling changes on which benefits realisation from investment in ICT systems is dependent; and
- Right to left - the strategic drivers and investment objectives to which the benefits will contribute.

An interesting variation comes from Victoria in Australia where an Investment Logic Map reverses the BDN mapping as follows:

- the drivers and objectives to which benefits contribute are mapped from left to right; and
- the investment in enabling assets and business changes that combined, lead to the benefits identified above are mapped right to left.

The BDN methodology is illustrated by a simplified example as shown in Figure 2.

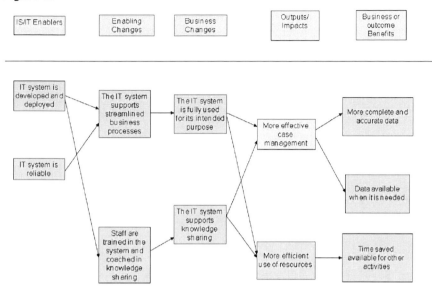

Figure 2: Benefits Dependency Network

These approaches can also be enhanced by considering the degree of confidence in the cause and effect chain based on:

- the existence, or otherwise, of evidence supporting the cause and effect proposition; and
- the possibility that factors outside the project may impact on benefit realisation.

This can be assessed as shown in Figure 3.

The advantage of this approach is that it improves our understanding of the logic underpinning an investment and the likelihood that we will be able to measure benefits realisation in practice – and this in turn informs the selection of appropriate measures and indicators (see below and Chapter 8).

In many ways what matters is not so much which approach to benefits modelling is used; in fact the most appropriate approach will depend on the circumstances, but the rigour with which the process is undertaken.

RAG matrix for assessing cause and effect		Possibility that factors outside the project impact on benefit realisation			
		High	Medium	Low	Nil
	Score	1	2	3	4
Empirical evidence support-ing cause and effect.	3	Red 3	Amber 6	Green 9	Green 12
Logical argument for cause and effect supported by some empirical evidence that is testable over time.	2	Red 2	Red 4	Amber 6	Amber 8
Logical argument for cause and effect but with little or no empirical evidence and testing the relationship is problematic.	1	Red 1	Red 2	Red 3	Red 4

Figure 3: Assessing confidence in benefits claims

Benefits practitioner workshops can be useful in this regard in ensuring that the models developed are sound. They also have an added advantage in that run well, they help build consensus around, and commitment to, a project and so improve the chances of benefits realisation. Key factors to consider in developing a benefits workshop include:

Membership – this should include IT professionals, project team members and subject matter experts (including users) from the business. Those present need to have the expertise to identify the potential business benefits from the ICT project or programme.

Authority to act – those present should be empowered to represent their organisational constituency and to agree the resulting analysis.

Length – experience shows that whilst it may be tempting to try to cover everything in one go, anything more than two hours can be counter productive. Better to hold a series of workshops than risk disengaging key stakeholders. The Investment Logic Map used by the Victorian government referred to above is, for example, the output from a series of three, two hour workshops focusing on: problem definition; solution definition; and benefits definition.

Format/content – the workshop should encompass five key stages:

1. Introductions – so everyone knows who everyone else is and which organisational constituency they represent.
2. Purpose – to develop a shared understanding of the objectives of the workshop i.e. to identify the benefits of the project or programme and the cause and effect chain underpinning the realisation of those benefits and any required business changes. Consideration of scale of impact may also be covered or may be explored after the workshop.
3. Background briefing – including the strategic context of the project and the key functionality to be provided.
4. Benefits Mapping – participants identify the key elements in the benefits map. For example, if the OGC's 'Managing Successful Programmes' approach is used, the enablers, intermediate and end benefits. Where Benefits Dependency Networks are used, this analysis will need to be augmented by identification of any enabling (i.e. one off) and business changes (recurring changes) upon which benefits realisation will depend.
5. Conclusions, actions arising and next steps. This should include, at a minimum, the date by which the model will be converted into electronic format (using Visio for example) and circulated to participants for validation.

Organisational issues – the effectiveness of the workshop can be severely limited if attendees dip in and out to address work issues or to take phone calls. Holding the workshop 'off site' or at least requiring mobiles to be turned off is therefore essential. Also make sure that you have a sufficient supply of benefits mapping 'tools' – brown paper, blu tack (to attach the brown paper to the walls), post it notes (to capture the key elements in your chosen modelling approach) and coloured pens to record the benefits and to draw the linkages (potentially using red, yellow and green to represent confidence in each of the cause and effect linkages as outlined above).

Facilitation – I've put this last but this does not reflect its importance. Successful benefits modelling is highly dependent on a skilled and motivated facilitator. Her/his job is to ensure that the workshop achieves its objectives, whilst ensuring that everyone present is sufficiently involved. This calls for an active but impartial approach – active in the sense that the role requires that the workshop is steered towards its objectives, and impartial in the sense that the facilitator's role is to help the attendees reach a shared understanding of the investment logic, but not to impose her/his views on the group. A key aspect of the role is to play back the conclusions to the group at regular points throughout the workshop and to capture key decisions as they arise.

The output of the workshop and post workshop consultation should be an agreed benefits map. The next stage will quantify the scale of the benefits identified – this usually requires analysis including review of current performance information from the organisation's management information system. Where such relevant information is not available, baselining current performance and engaging with users to identify the scope for improvement is usually required. A follow up workshop may then be held to discuss and agree the scale of benefits forecast. One word of warning – there is a natural tendency for project representatives to be optimistic about the potential benefits and for business leads to be more pessimistic, although they'd say, realistic. This is natural because the project representatives will be keen to agree as many benefits as possible as this will help ensure funding for the project. On the other hand, the business representatives may know less about the project, but what they will know is that they will probably be held to account for the realisation of the benefits and so will be keen to agree more attainable targets. The challenge for the facilitator is therefore to achieve a balance between these two extremes – remembering that more benefits is not necessarily better, especially if those benefits are not realistic. Once benefits have been identified and quantified they need to be validated and it is to this that we now turn.

Stage 2 - Benefits Validation

Benefits modelling as outlined above is important because it helps make the implicit assumptions underpinning an investment explicit, and identify any gaps in the investment logic. Modellers are however subject to the same cognitive biases relating to over-confidence referred to in Chapter 1 when we were considering the causes of forecasting error. We therefore need to augment modelling with formal validation which represents a checkpoint against optimism bias and strategic misrepresentation. Validation should encompass: checks to ensure benefits claimed are consistent with the organisation's Benefits Eligibility Framework; formal adjustments for optimism bias; checks for overlaps with initiatives elsewhere in the organisation's change portfolio; and validation with the recipients. We consider each of these in turn before examining some of the general issues associated with validating efficiency and effectiveness benefits.

Step one is an independent review of the benefits claimed to ensure that they are consistent with the organisation's Benefits Eligibility Framework. This can be undertaken by the finance function, the Project and Programme Management Office / Centre of Excellence, or where one has been established, the Portfolio Management Office or Value Management Office. Far better than identifying inconsistencies in the business case, is a policy of getting it right first time – and this calls for clear communication with project teams and business case writers to explain the role and content of the Benefits Eligibility Framework. This should be supported by training sessions in the more complex and specialist aspects of the framework including benefits modelling. In this way compliance with the Benefits Eligibility Framework can be built into the business case development process. But just to be clear, this is more than just a test for technical compliance. The objective is to test the assumptions underpinning the benefits forecast by asking are they reasonable and what value will be realised? An 'Advocatus Diaboli' as recommended by Ayers (2007), or a Value Management Office (see Chapter 9) can play a role here in providing independent, expert scrutiny and challenge.

Step two is to consider whether any adjustments to the quantified benefits should be made for optimism bias. The HM Treasury Green Book says that, "*appraisers should make explicit adjustments for this bias. These will take the form of increasing estimates of the costs and decreasing, and delaying the receipt of, estimated benefits.*" The problem we immediately face is by how much should we decrease our benefits forecasts? The Green Book advises using either the cross-departmental guidance for generic project categories available on the HMT website or departments' own empirically based adjustments. But this does not really help us for, as we saw in Chapter 1, the research undertaken by Mott MacDonald into the scale of optimism bias was unable to produce reliable estimates for the scale of that bias in the case of benefits and, consequently, there are no generic adjustments. So unless organisations have their own empirically derived data on benefits realisation compared to benefits forecast on a reference class of similar projects, we have no obvious basis on which to adjust our forecasts - and experience indicates that few organisations have a statistically sound database (it is noted for example, that although the Department for Transport commissioned research in 2004 to determine relevant adjustments for optimism bias, as far as benefits were concerned, the researchers found they could not be estimated due to, "*lack of statistical data*"). Alternatives include: building in 'reality checks' in the development of benefits forecasts as discussed above; agreeing the benefits with the recipients (Step 4 below); and/or undertaking some form of confidence assessment as discussed under Benefits Realisation Planning below.

Step three is to understand whether the benefit identified might be affected by changes elsewhere in the organisation's portfolio of change. This includes checking by the Portfolio Management Office or PPM Centre of Excellence whether there are any planned or current projects that might impact on the benefits claimed. Additionally, senior management should also be asked to confirm that there are no envisaged strategic changes (including known legislative change) that would impact on the benefits case as set out.

Step four is to agree the benefits with the recipients – most usually, operational managers or business change managers in the relevant business unit. As has been stated above, this step more than any other helps ensure benefits are realisable by ensuring they are agreed with those who will be responsible for their realisation in practice <u>prior to investment</u>. Where the organisation has taken the step to recipient-based, or enterprise benefits realisation management, benefits claimed by projects should be reflected in the relevant organisational benefits realisation plans (see Chapter 9).

Example 2 – Agreeing benefits with the recipients

The CJS IT portfolio included projects that were forecast to deliver benefits to not only the sponsoring organisation, but also to other organisations across the system i.e. improvements in efficiency and effectiveness in one part of the system resulted in both direct and indirect benefits for organisations elsewhere in the system. For example, improved efficiency in court administration, scheduling and inter-agency communication helped reduce wasted police time attending court only to discover the case had been adjourned. A key learning was that getting agreement to these cross system benefits was problematic, particularly after the project had been funded. The response was to appoint Benefits Realisation Managers in each organisation responsible for agreeing the benefits forecasts to be realised by their organisation. This meant that project representatives had to engage with these Benefits Realisation Managers from across the criminal justice system in agreeing the scale and value of any benefits forecast. These Benefits Realisation Managers also met collectively as a Benefits Working Group to examine the overall benefits position, to challenge each other to do more, and to consider whether any actions were required to remove obstacles to greater benefits realisation across the system.

Beyond the above, there are specific considerations in relation to cross-organisation benefits, social value benefits, mandatory and infrastructure projects – these are considered separately in Chapters 4-7 because of their particular characteristics. Before that we consider validation in relation to two generic types of benefit: firstly effectiveness/performance improvement benefits, and then efficiency benefits.

Effectiveness/Performance or Strategic Benefits

Business cases often open with a list of the organisational strategies the project will support. We should take such claims with a pinch of salt for, as Sanwal (2007) says, this is, "*the justification of last resort or when an investment owner does not want to think about why to do an investment. In essence, strategy is the reason often cited when the benefits of a particular idea cannot be articulated in a more lucid manner.*"

The importance of this is highlighted in the National Audit Office/OGC's list of Common Causes of Project Failure where number 1 is, "*Lack of a clear link between the project and the organisation's key strategic priorities.*" A step in the right direction is an attempt at strategic alignment or fit, which maps the functionality delivered by a project to the organisation's strategic targets and business priorities with, for example, a high, medium or low impact rating. An alternative is to use the OGC's project rating categories to assess the scale of strategic alignment, see Figure 4.

Mission Critical	A. ESSENTIAL to the successful delivery of
	    i) a major legislative requirement OR
	    ii) a Public Service Agreement (PSA) target OR
	    iii) a major policy initiative announced and owned by the PM or a Cabinet Minister
	B. If the programme or project is not successful there are catastrophic implications for delivery of a key public service, national security or the internal operation of a public sector operation.

Highly Desirable	A. IMPORTANT (but not essential) for the delivery of:
	    i) a major legislative requirement OR
	    ii) a PSA target OR
	    iii) a major policy initiative announced and owned by the PM or Cabinet Minister
	B. ESSENTIAL to the successful delivery of
	    i) a minor legislative requirement OR
	    ii) a high profile (but not PSA) target OR
	    iii) other government policy initiatives
	C. If the programme or project is not successful there are serious (but not catastrophic) implications for the delivery of a key public service, national security, or the internal operation of a public sector organisation.
	D. If the programme or project is not successful there are catastrophic implications for the delivery of non-key public services or the realisation of business benefits.

Desirable	All programmes or projects that do not meet the mission critical or highly desirable criteria.

Figure 4: Assessing strategic alignment using the OGC ratings

39

But this doesn't tell us anything about how this impact will be achieved, when it will be realised, or what degree of confidence we can have in the claims. It is particularly important that we understand the benefit rationale in the case of strategic benefits because they are typically difficult to measure and attributing improvements to source initiatives after implementation is problematic – the time lags are often long with a multitude of factors affecting performance. Benefits modelling, as outlined above, is helpful in this regard as it demonstrates the cause and effect chain underpinning project benefits and the linkages can be extended (as in the BDN and Root Cause Modelling – see Chapter 4) to show the relationship between the benefits and investment objectives and strategic drivers. One approach that takes this a step further is Strategic Contribution Analysis which combines benefits modelling with strategy mapping as follows:

- Strategy Mapping – starting with the organisational Vision (the 'Where'), through the Strategies (the 'How') to the Measures (the 'What') used to assess success. The following example (Figure 5) has been compiled from the UK Government's 2007 Service Transformation Agreement.

- Benefits Mapping as outlined in Chapter 3, showing how ICT investments, and enabling and business changes, can be combined to realise benefits – and how these benefits contribute to the strategic metrics identified above.

When the two are combined we have a logic chain, bottom up from project to benefit, and top down from the organisation's vision and strategies to the measures of strategic success. The linkages between project benefits and strategic measures then provide a basis for assessing strategic contribution and for agreeing the means by which this contribution will be measured. Once mapped, these impacts should also be agreed with the organisation's strategic planners and included, where appropriate, in the organisation's strategic plans and performance targets. In this way, effectiveness benefits can be 'booked' in a similar way as efficiency benefits are booked in unit budgets and headcount targets.

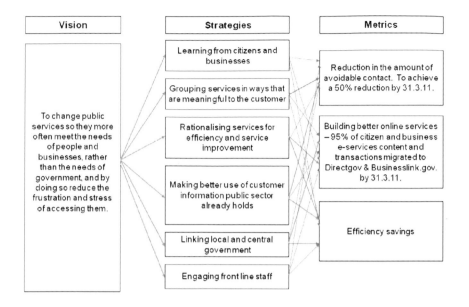

Figure 5: Strategy Mapping

Efficiency Benefits

We saw in the last chapter that efficiency benefits include cost and time savings and can be cashable or non-cashable. Whilst validating cashable benefits is usually relatively straight forward where such benefits are 'booked' in unit budgets, headcount targets or unit costs, there is one issue that needs to be addressed. Efficiencies need to be checked to ensure that they are actually realised in practice, rather than just cutting the budget i.e. that the budgetary savings have no adverse impact on output quantity or service quality.

Things are not quite so simple with regard to non-cashable time-based efficiency savings. Here four points must be kept in mind:

1. Firstly the value bought is <u>not</u> the time saving but what you can do with that time saving.

2. Following on from this, the benefit remains <u>potential</u> until resources are redeployed to other value-adding activity. The risk we face is that time savings may well be achieved, but unless action is taken to utilise this time effectively, the value of the time saved may be lost due to benefits 'leakage'. As one IT director is quoted by Gartner (2005) as saying, "*Sometimes projects have*

41

fallen short where benefits were reducing headcount. You can't physically take .3 of a head out." The result is that time savings are 'lost' either in time spent socializing or in proving Parkinson's Law that, *"work expands to fill the time available."* That's not to say that some value might be added, only that we won't be able to demonstrate this. In reality, the value realised is often significantly less than the potential. The importance of actively managing the realisation of value from non-cashable time savings is neatly captured in the following quote from Lerner (2002), a former strategic planner,

"We were survivors, dwellers forever in the cracks of the vast organisational chart. Disperse us, downsize us, squash us, transfer us, and we will reassemble someday, somewhere, to once again build new layers of redundancy, waste, and glaring irrelevance."

The trouble is that this is too often the situation we find with forecast time savings being 'lost' in the wider context of meeting business as usual pressures. The Benefits Profile and/or Realisation Plan (see below) should therefore address the issue of how time savings will be re-deployed to value adding activity and what measures will be used to assess this.

3.   Following on from the above, the value of the time saved is not the cost of that time but rather the value of the additional activities that can be undertaken in the time freed up. Whilst it is common practice to value time savings at the marginal gross salary cost, this is a dangerous policy with non-cashable benefits as it confuses the issue and diverts attention from managing the realisation of the benefit. In fact time savings are effectively a voucher – and in valuing such benefits it is worth bearing in mind that vouchers are only worth the face value if you use them. The reality is that in our personal lives we would not value a voucher at its face value, so why should we when it comes to valuing non-cashable efficiency benefits? The issue we face is what value to use, particularly when we are not certain what the time saved will be used for. One option is to use a conversion ratio accepting that not all the time saved will be re-deployed i.e. the time savings are multiplied by a factor ranging from 0 to 1 depending on the ability of the organisation to realise the time savings. Curley (2004) for example, suggests adjusting the time saved forecast to reflect two factors – firstly, the Hawthorne effect (*"the tendency of a group under study to over-perform"*), which may account for pilot studies over-estimating the potential time savings;

and secondly, that not all the potential time saved will be re-deployed to value-adding activity. Curley cites the adjustments used in a business case for wireless LAN technology in the City of Westminster Council where the time savings were divided by a half and then by half again – and it was this revised time saving that was used in valuing the benefit.

We need to be careful that where budgets are not reduced, there is no double counting between the non-cashable efficiency savings and the effectiveness benefits derived from those time savings i.e. where staff time is re-directed to other activities, one can count the benefit as either the value of the time saved or (preferably) the value of the performance improvement in the new area – but not both!

According to a report in the US for the NECCC (2005), Hillingdon Borough Council adopted a classification which distinguished between:

- *Red benefits* (hard cost reductions) which were estimated in terms of their monetary value.
- *Orange benefits* (time saving productivity benefits). These were modelled in two ways - in terms of their monetary value (by equating the time saved to the average salary rate) and in terms of the additional hours of time available to provide extra value-added services: and
- *Green (non-financial) benefits* that were not modelled as part of the financial appraisal, although they were considered as part of the overall justification for implementation.

4. One final consideration. Many organisations are required to develop and report progress against an efficiency plan - in such cases claimed efficiency benefits, cashable and non-cashable, should be agreed with those responsible for the organisation's efficiency plan and be 'booked' in that plan (although even where this is the case, the checks referred to above should still be undertaken to ensure the efficiencies are actually realised).

Stage 3 - Benefits Realisation Planning

So we've identified the potential benefits using benefits mapping or modelling and validated them via independent scrutiny and agreeing them with the recipients. The final stage is to bring it all together in a Benefits Realisation Plan that can be used to track the realisation of benefits in practice. But too often in practice we encounter one of two extremes:

43

- Verbose documents with grandiose claims about performance impact with no detail other than assertions about 'better', 'faster', and 'cheaper', but without any analysis that would indicate the scale of improvement or how it will be realised. Following the process outlined to date helps address this by ensuring the logic underpinning the benefits claimed is made explicit; or
- Detailed benefits analyses, but to such an extent that you cannot see the wood for the trees. More information is not necessarily better, particularly if it swamps the decision maker so that they are unable to ascertain whether and what action is required.

The answer, as always, is to keep it simple by applying the Pareto or 80:20 rule - focusing on the end benefits reflecting the primary investment objectives described in Chapter 1, and using a suite of standard benefits templates, plans and reports that provide a clear line of sight from benefits planning through to benefits realisation. The start point is the Business Case which should be completed in accordance with the Benefits Eligibility Framework. The Business Case should clearly identify the strategic drivers and investment objectives underlying the project, preferably in the form of a Strategy Map as outlined above, supported by a benefits model illustrating the logic underpinning the claims made – and ideally, combining them via Strategic Contribution Analysis.

Each of the major benefits should then have a Benefits Profile completed. This provides a single repository for the key information related to each material benefit – it's classification (efficiency or effectiveness and cashable or non-cashable); the trajectory and scale of impact; any dependencies and assumptions; who is responsible for realising the benefit; the business changes required to realise the benefits; and the measures that will be used to track realisation.

Once the Benefit Profiles are completed, the benefits can be prioritised and summarized in a Benefits Realisation Plan to focus management attention on the benefits of greatest value. This plan should include:

- A summary of the key benefits – their scale and the trajectory (ramp up schedule) for their realisation;
- Benefits maps to demonstrate the cause and effect chain underpinning benefits claims as well assessments of confidence in each benefit being realised;
- Details of any process changes and impacts on staff (training, skills, competencies) on which benefits realisation is dependent;

- Explicit details on how time savings will be realised – as an OGC case study of benefits management in the DVLA (2005) says, "*Delivery of project headcount reductions must be accompanied by an operational resource planning process that restricts the un-controlled migration of staff to other work.*";
- Governance arrangements including responsibility for business changes, realising benefits, reporting and addressing issues that arise, as well as arrangements for formal benefits reviews. Clear responsibility for benefit realisation is crucial – Ward and Taylor (1996) recommend that, "*Any benefits lacking such ownership should be removed from the list.*"; and
- How the way benefits will be tracked and reported – including the data sources to be used, who will collect the data, how often and what measures and indicators will be used.

The issue of measuring and tracking benefits is covered in more detail in Chapter 8, but for the time being it is only necessary to note that the identification of appropriate benefits can be assisted by adopting a bene-fits measurement taxonomy such as one derived from the benefits classi-fication framework outlined in Chapter 2.

Benefit type	Measures and Indicators	Measure/Indicator type
Efficiency cashable	Budget reductions	Quantitative financial
	Lower unit cost	Quantitative financial
Efficiency op-portunity value	Time re-deployed to other activities	Quantitative non-financial
	Activity measure in the area to which resources have been re-deployed i.e. what differences has the re-deployment of re-sources made?	Quantitative non-financial
	Value of time saved	Quantitative economic
Effectiveness	Leading and lagging indicators relevant to the area of per-formance Impacted	Quantitative and Qualitative non-financial
	Value of improved perform-ance	Quantitative economic
Cost avoidance	Money re-cycled to fund the project running costs	Quantitative financial
	Operating Budget reductions	Quantitative financial
	Indicators of what the money saved has been used for.	Quantitative economic or non-financial or Qualitative.

Figure 6: A Benefits Measurement Taxonomy

This taxonomy can be enhanced by incorporating an assessment of the quality of the measure/indicator in terms of the relationship between the indicator and the benefit that is to be tracked i.e. how confident are we that a change in the measure or indicator reflects realisation of that benefit – for example:

- **Green:** a direct and proportionate relationship between the benefit and measure used i.e. a change in the benefit is reflected in a change of the same scale in the measure used to evaluate realisation of that benefit.

- **Amber:** a logical relationship exists between the benefit and the indicator that can ideally be tested so that we have a reasonable degree of confidence that a change in the measure or indicator reflects a change in the benefit under review, although the scale of the change may be uncertain.

- **Red:** a logical relationship between the benefit and the indicator exists, but that relationship is indirect and a change in the indicator may not reflect a change in the underlying benefit under review. Indicators used to assess intangible benefits may well fall into this category. In such cases it is recommended that if the benefit is material, more than one indicator is used to provide enhanced confidence in benefits realisation.

This confidence framework can also be combined with that outlined earlier under Benefits Modelling in relation to confidence in the cause and effect chain.

The advantages of a benefits measurement taxonomy and confidence assessment, are that the treatment of benefits is consistent, not only in the classification of benefits, but also in the measures and indicators used to track the realisation of those benefits. It therefore aids comparisons both over time and between projects. The use of confidence factors also helps address the problems associated with gaming and appearance manipulation referred to in Chapter 1. Ultimately the approach to measuring and tracking benefits should be identified in the Benefits Profile and Benefits Realisation Plan and this should be agreed with the managers who will be responsible for realising the benefits identified. This is considered in more detail in Section 3. For the time being we turn to consideration of the particular issues associated with cross-departmental projects, social and citizen benefits, mandatory and infrastructure projects.

Section 1. Summary

We have seen that optimism bias and strategic misrepresentation is an empirical reality – benefits are regularly overstated, and often deliberately so. Addressing 'benefits fraud' calls for:

1. A consistent Benefits Eligibility Framework and classification system to provide a sound basis for benefits forecasting and to facilitate a level playing field for comparing investments and tracking benefits over time.

2. Validation checks to ensure the logic underpinning benefits claims is sound, that they are consistent with the Benefits Eligibility Framework and that recipients agree to realise them.

3. Above all, clarity and a shared understanding about what benefits you are buying from each ICT project or programme.

4. Recognizing that time savings are effectively vouchers – they only have a value when resources are re-deployed to other value-adding activity. Apply a conversion ratio that recognises that not all this value will be realised.

5. Sound approaches to benefits identification built on benefits modelling, participative benefits workshops and Strategic Contribution Analysis that link project benefits to the organisation's strategies.

6. Effective planning for realisation in the form of Benefits Profiles and a Benefits Realisation Plan encompassing how and when benefits will be realised, responsibility and accountabilities for their realisation, and responsibility for any business changes on which benefits realisation depends.

Section 2
Capturing all forms of value

"I love money more than the things it can buy... but what I love more than money is other people's money."
Lawrence Garfield in 'Other People's Money'

After reading this Section you will:

- Understand why it is important that we capture all forms of value from our portfolio of ICT projects and programmes.

- Have an appreciation of practical solutions to identifying and measuring all forms of value i.e. augmenting the efficiency and effectiveness benefits identified in the previous section with:

  - benefits in cross-departmental settings;
  - citizen benefits and wider social value;
  - mandatory projects and the value of the avoidance of 'things gone wrong'; and
  - the potential opportunity value inherent in infrastructure investments.

So far in our benefits management journey we have focused on ensuring that the benefits claims made in business cases, benefits plans and project appraisals are robust and realisable. This ensures that we have some confidence that the data used to inform our investment decisions is sound and will provide a solid basis on which to manage the realisation of these benefits in practice. So far so good, but we also need to ensure that our benefits cases are complete i.e. that all potential benefits are recognised or 'captured'.

This is important because firstly, without an understanding of the full potential benefits of an initiative, investment decisions may be distorted. Investments are usually made on the basis of relative anticipated value derived from the cost required i.e. potential initiatives compete for available funds and investment in one area has an opportunity cost in terms of other initiatives that are denied funding or are delayed. This can in turn damage organisational performance and the quality of services provided if we invest in low value projects and so deny or delay investment in more value-adding projects.

Secondly, capturing all potential benefits lays the basis for value creation. The reality is that most benefits don't just happen, they need to be 'harvested' – processes need to be re-engineered, jobs re-designed, or resources re-allocated. There is therefore a real risk that if you don't capture all potential value then potential benefits will just drain away.

Thirdly, recognising and managing all potential benefits provides the basis for organisational learning about what works, how benefits are realised and what has the greatest impact in practice – and this knowledge can in turn be used to inform future investments and the investment appraisal and benefits management processes themselves.

Lastly, we are usually investing somebody else's money whether it is taxpayers' money in the public sector, or shareholders' money in the private sector – hence the quote at the start of this Section from the film 'Other People's Money'. Accountability therefore calls for some evidence that we have invested this money wisely – and that means being able to demonstrate all the value created from that investment.

It is therefore essential that we recognise all forms of value in our business cases, investment appraisals and benefit management regimes. The benefits modelling techniques already discussed are of help here in identifying potential efficiency and effectiveness benefits, but there are also some types of benefit that are worthy of specific consideration. They include:

- benefits that cross organisational boundaries (see Chapter 4);
- forms of value that are peculiar to the public sector such as benefits to citizens and to wider society (see Chapter 5);
- benefits derived from mandatory projects (see Chapter 6); and
- the potential, or options value, implicit in infrastructure investments (see Chapter 7).

In each of these areas there are factors which make demonstrating value problematic. In the following chapters we consider each of the above in turn before we bring everything together in the last Section with some thoughts on how we can mobilize ourselves to realise the forecast benefits and to create additional value.

Chapter 4
Cross-organisational Benefits

"Every kind of peaceful cooperation among men is primarily based on mutual trust and only secondarily on institutions such as courts of justice and police."

Albert Einstein

Introduction

Realisation of benefits in a cross-organisational setting is problematic in that benefits to one organisation may well be dependent on business change elsewhere in the system. A report from the Cabinet Office to the OECD in 2006 noted that in respect of eGovernment, *"Business cases were found to be particularly strong on the assessment of costs and benefits to the lead department; however the identification and quantification of external benefits i.e. to users or other departments, was less strong, resulting in business cases that often understated benefits and provided an incomplete base for tracking future third-party benefits through to realisation."*

We consider the issue of user benefits in due course, but first we address the issue of realising benefits across departmental boundaries. The challenge that we face here is firstly to articulate these benefits, and then to lay the basis for their realisation. This in turn requires a joint benefits planning and realisation process based on:

- active participation by subject matter experts from all organisations affected;
- workshops to articulate, agree and quantify forecast benefits and the logic underpinning them;
- detailed analysis to explore the business changes required to realise the benefits forecast;
- integration of the forecast benefits into the benefits management regime to ensure that agreements on forecasts are carried through to realisation. This in turn requires accountability arrangements that cross departmental boundaries to address the issue where investment in one organisation is required to realise benefits in another part of the overall system; and
- trust - ultimately realisation of cross-organisational benefits depends on trust based on a shared commitment to improving the system as a whole, even if it's at the short term expense of one part of it.

Clearly the exact mechanisms used will vary with the situation, but we explore these principles by examining the approach adopted in the CJS IT portfolio.

Example 3 - The Combined Effectiveness Impact benefits and the Root Cause Model

The CJS IT portfolio encompassed three government departments (the Home Office, Ministry of Justice and Attorney General's Department) and seven criminal justice organisations (the Police, Crown Prosecution Service, Crown and Magistrates Courts, Prison and Probation Services, and Youth Justice). Because these organisations operate as part of a wider criminal justice system, changes in one have effects, both intended and unintended, elsewhere in the system. As noted by the Cabinet Office in the quote above, the business cases for the individual projects and programmes, which had in several cases been prepared prior to the formation of the portfolio, were found to be relatively strong on the efficiency benefits forecast to be realised by the sponsoring organisations, but they were less robust in terms of their impact on the effectiveness of the system as a whole – to the extent that where such benefits were recognised in the business cases, the scale of impact was generally unquantified or unsupported by any reliable or consistent form of empirical research or logical cause and effect analysis. There was consequently no way in which this impact could be assessed to determine whether it had been realised, or any basis for determining whether additional action was required. This was a major shortcoming and failed to reflect the reality that implementing modern infrastructure, case management systems and enabling information sharing by investment in ICT-enabled business change, had massive potential - not only in saving money and time, but more significantly, in improving the effectiveness of the system as a whole in terms of: bringing more offenders to justice, improving services to witnesses and victims, and reducing re-offending.

The approach adopted was to complete a 'Root Cause Model' to articulate, quantify and as a basis for valuing the impact of the portfolio as a whole on the major problems and issues within the criminal justice system – and because these benefits resulted from the combined contribution of several projects, they were termed, 'Combined Effectiveness Impact' benefits.

The approach consisted of the following six stages:

1. The key problems and issues in the system (or what are termed 'Consequences' in the model) were identified and agreed. These

---

included: re-offending; ineffective trials; inappropriate time in custody post trial; offences committed on bail; inappropriate prosecution decisions; unnecessary witness attendance at court; offender self harm and harm to others; unpaid fines; detections; victim and witness care; and enforcement of arrest warrants.

2. Research was undertaken to ascertain the root causes of these 'Consequences' and this analysis was agreed with subject matter experts from the respective agencies.

3. Interactive workshops were then held with the subject matter experts, practitioners and project representatives to consider the impact of the portfolio as a whole and its constituent projects and programmes, on the root causes of the identified consequences. This analysis was documented graphically (originally in Visio but later using a specialist software package) in a series of cause and effect maps for each 'Consequence'. The Root Cause Model therefore represents a detailed cause and effect chain from project functionality through to contribution to organisational targets. This analysis was agreed with the benefits managers from each organisation.

4. The Root Cause Model was also underpinned by cost and measurement data that enabled the performance impacts forecast by the model to be quantified in case or percentage terms, and also to be valued in economic terms using standard costs where available.

5. 'Consequences' were allocated to the agency representative agreed as having greatest influence over that part of the system and the Portfolio Unit then worked with these representatives to track and analyse benefits realisation. Relevant benefits were thus included in the standard benefits planning and reporting regime of each agency and as part of the overall portfolio-level benefits reporting – with benefits profiles being agreed that were in turn also validated by the departmental efficiency and strategic planners. In this way, these 'Combined Effectiveness Impact' benefits were subject to similar validation and tracking mechanisms as the benefits delivered from sponsor organisation projects.

6. Forecasts were reviewed and revised on a quarterly basis to reflect the latest data on system performance and project delivery. The model was also refreshed as new projects joined the portfo-

lio and as new learning about the impact of initiatives was identified.

Beyond providing a basis for forecasting the quantified impact of the CJS IT portfolio on the effectiveness of the criminal justice system as a whole, the approach was found to have a number of additional advantages in providing:

- an effective method of mapping from initiative through to Public Service Agreement (PSA) targets and communicating this impact to stakeholders;
- a consistent method for forecasting effectiveness and efficiency benefits across the portfolio;
- an adaptable approach to benefits identification – as new projects came on stream the model was revised to reflect their forecast impact on system performance;
- an effective check against double counting – where several projects were forecast to impact on system performance, the model enabled benefits claimed to be validated and double counting to be stripped out at the portfolio level;
- a means to improve cross-system understanding by promoting discussion and consideration of the consequences of changes in one part of the system on other parts of the system;
- an improved understanding of how projects can impact on performance and what business changes were necessary to realise those benefits; and
- finally, it also provided a basis for articulating and quantifying the social value attributable to the portfolio – and it is to this aspect of value capture that we now turn in Chapter 5.

Chapter 5
Public Value

"Consumer expectations of Government services as well as others are rising remorselessly...They see the revolutionary effect of IT and want it applied across the public sector too. And above all else, the majority today are taxpayers. Government money is their money. They expect a return."

Tony Blair

Introduction

The focus of this book so far has been on realising value from the investment in ICT irrespective of organisational setting. Whilst the practical examples have been drawn in the main from the public sector, many of the principles and practices covered to date are equally applicable to (and in some cases are derived from) the private sector. We now consider some benefits management issues that are specific to the public sector.

Investments in the public sector differ from those in the private sector in several ways:

- the investment justification is often to meet some social objective (public safety, environmental sustainability, public health etc) rather than to achieve a financial return;
- these social objectives can be difficult to measure reliably and this is complicated by the issue of attribution – even if we can measure an outcome it is often difficult in practice to attribute any change to a specific initiative given the multitude of factors affecting these outcomes;
- conversely, interventions can have unanticipated benefits. For example, an experiment in New York (Friedman, 1997) aimed at reintegrating offenders and drug addicts into the community found little impact on arrest rates (the intended objective of the programme), but the treatment group did achieve higher employment earnings and reduced reliance on social services which justified the economic investment in the programme;
- the beneficiaries (the citizen) often do not pay directly for the service received and the absence of a pricing mechanism makes valuing benefits problematic;
- in many cases, the beneficiaries of initiatives include not only those directly 'served' but also wider society – for example, an

55

effective education system is of value beyond those in the class-room;

- the public sector generally cannot choose which market seg-ments to target – services such as health, education and justice are generally universal in provision; and
- the timespan for evaluating the full impact of initiatives such as improvements in education and public health, can extend over many years.

Accepting the difficulties in measuring value, it is nevertheless crucial that this is addressed for four reasons. Firstly, as stated at the start of this Section, we are not investing our own resources – it's taxpayers' money, and this calls for a degree of accountability based on an under-standing of the basis on which we are making investments. In short, we need to know what outcomes are expected and have some means for determining whether they have been achieved.

Secondly investments should only be made when the benefits (in terms of financial savings; improved services to the citizen; and attainment of social outcomes) exceed the costs. If we cannot reliably and consistently appraise the value to be created we have no effective means of prioritis-ing our investments or for determining that the potential benefits justify the cost of the investment. The linked point is that public resources are limited, and consequently investment in projects where the value created does not justify the investment also has an opportunity cost in denying or delaying funding to other potentially value-adding initiatives.

Thirdly, in an increasingly fiscally constrained environment, funding is dependent on our ability to demonstrate a positive return on investment – not necessarily in financial terms, but in showing that the value of the benefits however that is defined, exceeds or justifies the cost required. The reality is that as funding gets tighter, so there is likely to be an in-creased focus on business cases demonstrating that the potential 'bang' is worth the 'buck' required to generate that 'bang'. One study by the NECCC in the United States in 2002 for example, concluded that, "*the use of economic business cases will become more important*" with decreasing use of non-economic cases relying on qualitative benefits. A report for the US General Service Administration a year later noted that the E-Government workgroup of the EU had found, "*unconditional support for E-Government is being replaced by a growing demand for projects to create value and deliver Return on Investment.*" Paul Wormeli (2006) agrees, "*Anecdotal data is no longer an acceptable basis for making ma-jor funding decisions. While this principle has been and will continue to be violated by pressures felt in legislative bodies, the mainstream pro-*

gram evaluation and budget justification trend is toward clear data supporting the efficacy of programs to be funded."

Lastly, the public sector does not have a good track record in demonstrating a return on investment in major IT-enabled business change. We noted in the Introduction that the Public Accounts Committee commented in 1999 that, *"for more than two decades, implementing IT systems successfully has proved difficult ... implementation of IT systems has resulted in delay, confusion and inconvenience to the citizen and, in many cases, poor value for money to the taxpayer."* More recently the OGC reported in its Gateway News (December 2003) that, *"Deficiencies in benefits capture bedevils nearly 50% of government projects."*

This issue is not restricted to the UK:

- In 2006 the OECD reported that, *"The United States federal government will spend over USD 60 billion on ICT technology and systems in 2006. This huge expenditure has led many to ask if ICT investment is providing more than USD 60 billion in value to government agencies and, ultimately, tax payers. The answer is increasingly that nobody knows."*
- The same OECD report referred to above also reported similar problems in Australia, *"Data from Australia on achieved benefit/cost ratios [in] central government indicates that rates of return on ICT investments often are low or negative."*; and
- In Europe, the eGovMoNet study that commenced in 2008 stated, *"The Implementation of eGovernment solutions is expected to bring a number of advantages including efficiency, increased user satisfaction, and reduction of administrative burden. However, this cannot be taken for granted any longer. Well informed strategic decisions on investments in eGovernment developments will need measurements of impact and user satisfaction."*

Unless we can demonstrate the value created, continued funding may be put at risk – as was reported by Cresswell et al in 2006 when the Senate Appropriations Committee recommended no funding for the administration's 2007 e-government program because, *"the committee has no confidence that the amounts being assessed have any relationship to the benefits anticipated"*.

The problem is often not that the potential value is not there, but that it is not recognised and is consequently not managed. The issue we face is that financial cost-benefit and return on investment metrics are not always well suited to the public sector. The eGEP report for the European Commission in 2006 for example, concluded that, "*traditional ROI investment measures do not fully account for the value from e Government, since many of its benefits are non-financial and qualitative/intangible and contribute to a greater social value than can be measured using only financial and quantifiable indicators."* A study undertaken for the Australian Government NOIE in 2003 similarly concluded that, "*Determining the benefit/cost ratio for e-Government is not straightforward, as the outcomes and benefits are not just financial."* But it is crucial that we have ways of reliably assessing and quantifying this non-financial social value if we are to realise the greatest impact from our investment of taxpayer's money, demonstrate that we have done so, and thus justify continued investment.

Despite the problems outlined above, there is a way forward. Mark Moore's work (1995) on the concept of Public Value provides a basis for capturing the wider aspects of value and this has influenced thinking on both sides of the Atlantic as well as in Australia. Moore identified three forms of Public Value:

- Outcomes such as a sustainable environment, public safety, low unemployment, public health, and reduced poverty.

- Services – such as education, health and justice. Importantly, value is seen as deriving from not only the quality of the service itself, but also the citizen's experience of the service. Research by Kearns for the IPPR in the UK (2004) reports that perceptions of service quality are driven by five underlying factors: availability (not just to the person but also to others, particularly the most vulnerable members of society); user satisfaction (in turn driven by factors such as quality of customer service experience, level of information available, the degree of choice and convenience and staff advocacy); perceived importance of the service; fairness in provision; and cost.

- Trust - or public confidence with, and participation in, the democratic process.

Whilst these forms of value are independent they can also be linked – for example as Kelly and Muers (2002) note, reports of reductions in crime can improve trust in Government and satisfaction with the police whether or not the police were primarily responsible for the reduction in crime in the first place.

Moore does not argue that economic investment appraisal is inappropriate, indeed there is an obligation on government to provide services as cost-effectively as possible, but rather that economic appraisal needs to be augmented by appraisal that takes into consideration wider aspects of public value and citizens' needs, wants and desires. The good news is that progress has been made in this regard in several jurisdictions and methodologies and frameworks developed in the United States, Australia and Europe all take a more holistic view of the concept of value than the traditional financial metrics. We explore this by briefly examining three of the major frameworks below.

The US Value Measuring Methodology

In 2001, Booz Allen Hamilton in association with Harvard University's Kennedy School of Government, undertook a study sponsored by the Social Security Administration and the General Services Administration. The objective was to identify a methodology for measuring the value of e-Government initiatives unaccounted for by traditional cost-benefit and return on investment methodologies. The findings were published in 2002 and concluded, "*The full value of an e-service must be measured from multiple perspectives...it cannot be captured in a single internal financial metric (i.e. ROI)."*

The Federal Government developed the approach further and published revised guidelines, incorporating the lessons learned from applying the approach in practice, in a 'Highlights' document and 'How-To-Guide'. The resulting 'Value Measuring Methodology' (VMM) is based on consideration of five value factors, encompassing both tangible and intangible benefits, cost and risk. The five value factors are:

1. <u>Direct user (customer) value</u> - Benefits directly realised by users or multiple user groups, for example, time saved, more convenient service delivery/access etc.

2. <u>Social (non-direct user/public) value</u> – Benefits not related to direct users (society as a whole) for example, improved trust in government, participation, and inclusiveness.

3. <u>Government Operational/Foundational value</u> - improvements realised in current government operations and processes or those that lay the groundwork for future initiatives. For example, enterprise architecture and improved infrastructure.

4. Government Financial value - Financial benefits that have a direct impact on organisational (government service provider) and other federal government budgets via increased revenue, reduced costs or costs avoided.

5. Strategic/Political value - Benefits that move an organisation, and government as a whole, closer to achieving its strategic goals and mission.

The VMM therefore uses multi-criteria analysis (as does the Australian D&VAM examined below) to appraise potential investments in eGovernment and takes into consideration both financial and non-financial benefits, quantitative and qualitative aspects of value, and benefits realised by government organisations as well as those delivered to specific groups of citizens and wider society.

The value factors are prioritised by allocating weightings, reflecting senior management's priorities and the relative importance of each factor to the organisation. For example, according to Foley (2006), NASA used the VMM to examine options for the Geospatial Interoperability Office and the value weightings selected reflect the priority given to social and user value.

Value Factor	Weighting
Social	28.7
Direct User	26.5
Government Foundation	24.4
Government Financial	11.6
Strategic/Political	8.8

Figure 7: NASA Geospatial Interoperability Office Value Weightings

In each case sub-criteria and quantifiable performance measures are identified and prioritised - further details on the measures used in relation to direct user and social value are shown below. Normalised scales are used allowing objective and subjective measures of value to be combined into a single decision metric. It should also be noted that a 'bang for your buck' assessment can be accommodated by dividing the resulting value score by the cost, so enabling the value for money of different options to be appraised.

The Australian 'Demand and Value Assessment Methodology' (D&VAM)

This methodology was developed for the Australian Government Information Management Office (AGIMO) by DMR consultants. It distinguishes between 'benefits' which it defines as, "*an outcome whose nature and value...are considered advantageous to an organisation*" and 'value' which is seen as, "*the broader, collective term for the longer term contribution to the business goals and strategies*".

The assessment starts with an assessment of demand in which the service is assessed from the viewpoint of the end user. It then moves on to the value assessment, encompassing, as with the VMM, five forms of value:

1. Agency benefits/value - operating cost reductions, increased revenue, improved efficiency and productivity savings, improved effectiveness, and improved service or cycle times.

2. Strategic value - how well the initiative is aligned with the most important outcomes (and political objectives) for the organisation.

3. Consumer financial benefits - time and cost savings, faster payments and revenue generation opportunities to users of a service.

4. Social benefits - including improved quality of life; improved decision making; and more integrated delivery so increasing business opportunities.

5. Governance value - contribution to broader whole-of-government objectives including more open and inclusive government (citizen participation), accountability and improved information availability (transparency).

This is combined with assessments of risk to programme delivery and to achievement of benefits, to provide a simple but comprehensive assessment of value that is graphically presented in the form of a radar chart or spider diagram.

The eGovernment Economics project

In Europe, the methodology developed by the European Commission's 2006 e-Government Economics Project (e GEP) identified value in constituency and political value terms, as well as the more traditional agency-based efficiency and effectiveness categories. The framework developed is supported by a suite of 92 indicators covering the dimensions of efficiency, effectiveness and governance.

What we see from these frameworks (as well as others such as MAREVA in France and *WiBe 4.0* in Germany) is a common recognition that demonstrating the full value of public sector investment in ICT requires that we take account of benefits to individual and groups of citizens as well as the wider dimension of social value. This in turn requires a three stage approach: firstly, categorizing the potential sources of value, secondly quantifying them, and thirdly, valuing them where possible and required. We examine this approach in relation to the benefits to individuals and groups of citizens before considering the issue of wider social value.

Identifying and Quantifying User/Citizen benefits

The HM Treasury advice on measuring eGovernment benefits (2003) is that, "*Business case authors will need to consider customer (i.e. non-exchequer) costs and benefits as part of the option review.*" A checklist produced by the OECD (2006) can be useful in this regard. Derived from the HM Treasury and US VMM guidance, this checklist (see Figure 8) classifies user benefits into three categories - monetary benefits, time-based non-monetary benefits, and value-based non-monetary benefits.

Monetary benefits
Price reduction of charged-for service, avoidance of future price increases
Reduced cost of transmitting information by phone, post, paperless interactions, etc.
Reduced travel costs
Reduced associated costs (*e.g.* professional advice, software tools, equipment, etc., predominantly for businesses)
Revenue generating opportunities for citizens, businesses and intermediaries
Time-based non-monetary benefits
Reduced user time (hours saved)
Reduced need for multiple submission of data for different services and events
Reduced travel time
Reduced user time (hours saved)
Value-based non-monetary benefits
Quicker response
Reduced application processing time (elapsed time saving)
Improved response time to events
Improved interactive communication, particularly between government and remote communities
Improved information
More reliable and up-to-date

Faster and easier access
Transparency (e.g. status of live applications)
Can be live or real time
Enhanced democracy and empowerment
Improved reliability
Reduced error rates
Greater confidence and certainty of transaction
Service consistency
Overall reliability
Choice and convenience
Range of access channels, increased choice and ease of access
Greater user convenience (24/7 service delivery)
Decrease in abandoned transactions and complaints
Premium service
Extra tools and functionality for users
Improved customer service
Personalised service
Service integration

Figure 8: OECD Checklist – Benefits to users

This classification provides a useful starting point for identifying potential user benefits, but actually quantifying these benefits requires that we consider benefits from the user's perspective and this starts with the design of the initiative and the preparation of the business case. This requires that, as recommended by Sir David Varney's Service Transformation Review (2006), we bring private sector 'Voice of the Customer' (VoC) practices into public sector service design and delivery. The US VMM for example, requires that metrics be identified for each user group that reflect, "*what customers and stakeholders want and is important to them*" and this requires, "*Structured, facilitated, focused discussion.*" The Direct User Value measures used in the NASA case study were for example as shown in Figure 9 (note that the weightings total to the 26.5% weighting allocated to Direct User Value above):

Measure	Description	Weightings
Ease of Use	Geospatial resources and systems are easy to translate, transform, and ingest	9.81%
Metrics	Expertise required to support data transmission	
	Field mappings: number of semantic changes required to pass data	
	Complexity of data: number of changes in Field Length/Value/Types/etc	
Broad Data-Sharing Capabilities	Capabilities exist for broad GI data-sharing between communities of interest	6.63%

Measure	Description	Weightings
Metrics	Level of Effort required to support data transmission	
	Number of inquires for meta –data	
Data Availability and Accessibility	Geospatial data and applications are readily available and accessible for communities of interest	10.07%
Metrics	Is the data available in real time?	
	Number of hits (per day/hour/etc)	
	Number of downloads (per day/hour)	
	Are data available via inter- or intranet?	

Figure 9: NASA Geospatial Interoperability Office User Value Measures and Weightings

Techniques for achieving insight into, and understanding of, user needs, wants and desires include:

- Segmentation i.e. breaking users into groups with common characteristics to explore and gain customer insight via focus groups, interviews and surveys. Skilled questioning is often required to elicit unspoken needs and wants. The resulting insight should be used in designing the solution, for forecasting the scale of demand and, in due course, in evaluating whether those needs and wants have been met. The Australian D&VAM guidance for example, encourages users (including citizens, businesses, and intermediaries) to be involved in the assessment and evaluation of performance via focus groups;

- HMT eGovernment guidance (2003) also suggests, "*Creating 'archetypes' can help bring customer types or segments to life by personalizing them as individuals. This process involves building up a detailed picture of a 'typical' person with a name, home, family and friends, occupation, income, lifestyle preferences, attitudes, etc. This can help prompt ideas about needs.*" A similar approach involves workshops with participants putting themselves into the customer's position using role playing;

- Customer journey mapping which describes the customer experience of a service or set of services from need to outcome. As we shall see in Chapter 9, stories can prove a powerful means of engaging both hearts and minds, and customer journey mapping is a useful tool in this regard. Guidance from the Cabinet Office on customer journey mapping (2008) notes that, "*Mapping the ex-*

perience brings the story to life and engages your audience". In this way narrative is used to engage the user on an emotional level in the need for, and scope of, the change required to realise the potential benefits;

- Front line staff who engage with users on a regular basis can be a great source of data and information on users concerns and needs; and

- Market research to confirm the insight into customer needs is sound.

It is important to note that user needs and wants are not always obvious - as Mark Pearson, Head of Research at Egg is quoted as saying in the Cabinet Office's primer on customer insight, "*People can't always articulate what they want or need....You can't expect them to just give you the answers.*" One answer is ethnography which involves seeking to understand behaviour by observing users in real life situations. Cooper and Edgett (2007) point out that, "*If you want to study gorillas, a couple of focus groups with gorillas, an e-mail survey and a few interviews probably won't be enough. You must buy a tent and move into their village site – and camp out with them. And so it is with gaining real customer insights: You must move into their home, office or business and spend time observing and gaining insights.*"

The point is that by observing users in practice you can gain insights that just don't emerge from more formal consultation.

The output from this analysis of user needs should be a customer proposition which clearly describes the user needs and how the initiative will meet them i.e. in short, a clear articulation of the user perceived benefits.

Valuing User Benefits

As we have seen above, due in part to a tighter fiscal position, there is an increasing pressure to include all benefits in the Business Case – so beyond recognising and quantifying user benefits, how do we value them? Things are relatively straight-forward in relation to monetary benefits, but how do we value time and 'value based non-monetary' benefits? We will explore the issue of value-based benefits in a little more detail under the Social Value heading below, but at this point it is only necessary to note that contingent valuation techniques such as surveying people's willingness to pay and willingness to accept stipulated outputs or outcomes, can be used to provide a value in the absence of market prices.

As far as user time savings are concerned, HM Treasury guidance in the Green Book is that when valuing working time savings to businesses ('employers' time), the time saved should be valued at the gross wage rate plus non-wage labour costs (national insurance and pension contributions). In the case of time savings to citizens/non-business users ('own' time which can be working or non-working time), relevant guidance can be found in research into the value of travel time savings undertaken by Mackie et al (2003) for the Department for Transport (DfT). This recommends the use of standard values (averaged across income groups) modified where necessary for socio-economic status, rather than specific values for different groups. The research suggests standard rates for working time and non-working time as follows:

- Time savings in working time – the DfT research quotes rates of £17.44 per hour for car drivers and £25.17 per hour for rail passengers. HM Treasury eGovernment guidance (2003) also suggests that where more accurate estimates are difficult to obtain, a conservative estimate of £20 per hour for working time savings for customers at 2002 prices be used.
- Customer time savings in non-working time – a standard value of time saved averaged across all modes of transport of £3.74 per hour at 1998 values is quoted. The research also found that people value walking and waiting time more than car travel time and it is consequently recommended that the former be valued at twice the car driving rate.

It should be noted that there is some argument about the use of standard rates which do have theoretical shortcomings particularly in the assumption of equal marginal utility of time for all groups of users. In practice willingness to pay analysis could be undertaken for the various user groups but this can be expensive and there is always the risk of spurious accuracy. The Booz Allen Hamilton study that provided the basis for the US VMM for example, also strongly recommends that when time savings are monetarised a single rate for all citizens is used. The authors add that using higher rates for some, *"risks skewing services and raises questions of equitable treatment"*.

One final point - guidance on the approach to user benefits should be included in the organisation's Benefits Eligibility Framework as discussed in Chapter 2. This will help ensure a consistently sound approach is taken to forecasting citizen user benefits in investment cases and to tracking and measuring the realisation of these benefits in practice.

Social Value

The HM Treasury Green Book requires that, *"Wider social and environmental costs and benefits for which there is no market price also need to be brought into any assessment. They will often be more difficult to assess but are often important and should not be ignored simply because they cannot easily be costed'*. These benefits will obviously vary from service to service but some examples are identified in the HMT guidance on measuring the benefits of e-Government including the following, *"Benefits to Society/Nation"*.

	Benefits to Society/Nation
Monetisable benefits/efficiency savings	▪ More effective use of existing infrastructure ▪ Greater educational participation/retention/achievement ▪ Encourage socially/environmentally desirable behaviour (e.g. shift from road to public transport) ▪ Reduced regulatory burden/paperwork -> Economic development ▪ Stimulation of specific industry/sector.
Non-monetisable benefits	▪ Improved health ▪ Greater take-up of entitlements ▪ Enhanced democracy – increased user involvement / participation / contribution ▪ Greater Fairness and equality ▪ Leadership in digital economy ▪ Increased citizen well-being.

Figure 10. HMT Guidance - Benefits to society

Recognising these benefits is one thing, but quantifying and valuing them can be problematic – for example in the Criminal Justice context time savings from IT systems may be forecast with some certainty, but reductions in offending and improvements in public confidence are more difficult to measure and to attribute to a single initiative. A report from the OECD in 2006 reported that an Australian study found, *"little evidence of consistent frameworks being used to measure benefit/cost ratio, from a social benefit perspective"*. This lack of consistency in approach reflects the complexities involved - a study undertaken for the Australian Government's NOIE in 2003 concluded that, *"Determining the benefit/cost ratio for e-Government is not straightforward, as the outcomes and benefits are not just financial. A particular problem for agencies is in identifying and measuring social value."*

So how to progress? The HM Treasury Green Book suggests that in the absence of market prices, quasi-market prices can be elicited by contingent valuation techniques such as 'willingness to pay', where values are inferred from observed behaviour (revealed preferences) or by asking what people would be willing to pay for a particular benefit (stated preferences). In the case of costs, identifying what compensation people would require ('willingness to accept') can be used. We will not discuss these complex econometric measurement techniques here (readers that wish to explore these approaches in greater detail are referred to the HMT Green Book and the supplementary guidance: 'Managing Risks to the Public: Appraisal Guidance') other than to note that they are not without issues. For example, where people are not aware of the benefits it is difficult for them to say how much they would be willing to pay to receive them. Research has also identified inconsistencies between what people say in response to a questionnaire and their behaviour when faced with a choice in the real world. Flyvbjerg et al (2005) comment that, "*A problem with using stated causes is that what people say they do is often significantly different from what they actually do*". 'The Economist' noted in 1994 that Diamond and Hausman, "*cite evidence that the charitable donations people tell surveys they would make are up to ten times bigger than those they actually hand over.*"

One solution is to base contingent valuations on the views of experts – but again we quickly run into problems as experts are rarely without vested interests. Basing valuations on the views of a panel of experts and using the Delphi technique to reach a consensus, is therefore preferred to valuations derived from a single expert. Under this approach, consensus is obtained from a panel of experts over several rounds of anonymous questioning which enables the panel to revise their conclusions in the light of the views of others.

Because of the problems in valuing social benefits in monetary terms, some approaches make use of multi-criteria analysis in which relevant criteria are identified and quantified but not necessarily valued in monetary terms. We look at the approaches adopted by the US VMM and the Australian D&VAM in a little more detail, before reviewing two case studies from the Criminal Justice context where attempts were made to monetarise such value – one in the UK and one from Australia.

Measuring Social Value - the VMM and D&VAM

As outlined above, the US VMM includes Social (non-user) Value in its value framework. In deciding which aspects of social value to include in the appraisal, the VMM guidance advises that consideration be given to how extended the cause and effect chain is and the availability of reliable measures of impact - "*Organisations must determine whether future effects on social value are so far into the future that the cost and value of the analysis is minimal. For example, observation and measurement of the impact of improvements in the oil drilling permit issue process on the cost to drill and, ultimately, the consumer price for oil, [are] relatively straightforward. Relating the effect of a particular e-service such as on-line change of address filing, with a reduction of smog in a particular community is much more complicated, costly and time consuming. Would the result of that analysis be valuable to the decision maker? Probably not. Ultimately, determining which elements of social value to evaluate will be based on information derived from group discussions and posing the question to organisation management.*"

As with Direct User Value, measures for aspects of Social Value are identified and prioritised based on consultation with representative groups. The measures used in the NASA case study and their respective weightings totalling to the 28.7% weighting allocated to Social Value (see above) were:

- institutional effectiveness (5.74%);
- efficient use of taxpayer resources (3.73%);
- minimal barriers exist to finding and obtaining data (5.74%);
- citizens are able to make better decisions (7.75%); and
- extra-government coordination (5.74%).

In contrast to the approach adopted by the US VMM, the Australian D&VAM incorporates consideration of Social Value by assessing an initiative in terms of its:

- 'reach' in the context of the target group – scores of 1 to 5 are used where 1 represents less than 5% reach and 5 is more than 50%; and
- 'consequence' or the expected impact on the target social group. Again, scores range from 1 to 5, where 1 represents 'minimal impact' and 5, 'significant impact'.

The assessment of Governance value which encompasses changes in community participation, transparency and accountability is also based on reach and consequence ratings for target groups. These assessments are combined with the others contained within the D&VAM as outlined above.

Measuring Social Value – Criminal Justice

We conclude our consideration of the issue of social value by contrasting the approaches adopted in two programmes designed to facilitate information sharing in the criminal justice environment – the CJS IT portfolio in England and Wales and the IJIS programme in Queensland, Australia. Both cases sought not only to quantify social value but also to include this in the overall value proposition for the programme.

Example 4 – The CJS IT Approach to Wider Social Value

As we saw in Chapter 4, the Root Cause Model was developed to articulate and quantify the forecast impact of the CJS IT portfolio on major problems ('Consequences') in the Criminal Justice System. This analysis was also used to estimate the potential value of the CJS IT Portfolio on the economic and social cost of crime i.e. if the model indicated a value to the Criminal Justice System from reductions in re-offending or ineffective trials for example, then the value of this reduction to the public, specific groups such as victims, and public sector organisations that respond to the consequences of crime such as the National Health Service, could also be assessed. Specific benefits identified included:

- Time spent by offenders on bail provides them with the opportunity to commit further offences (Consequence 2). By improving information relating to supervision, monitoring and enforcement on bail and improving the decisions that are made when awarding bail, such offences may be reduced.
- Improved risk assessments and information sharing enables improved offender management and targeted interventions contributing to reduced re-offending (Consequence 12).
- Assuming that offenders are convicted more frequently as a result of improved detections (Consequence 14), and that some convictions lead to desistance from crime, then additional detections should shorten criminal careers and reduce the number of offences committed.
- Information sharing helps reduce the number of ineffective trials (Consequence 6) so realising time savings for people who attend court (including witnesses) or are involved in preparation for trials.

Independent economists were employed to quantify and value these benefits, using existing economic research such as Home Office Research Study 217 and OLR 30/05 into the scale and cost of crime and the number and cost of different categories of crime – violent, sexual, common

---

assault, robbery, burglary, theft and criminal damage.

The result was a series of forecasts of the social value to be derived from investment in projects within the CJS IT Portfolio. As always it is important that benefits claims are as robust as possible and in the case of social value benefits, this is particularly problematic – there are no representatives able to sign forecasts off on behalf of society or to evidence benefits realisation, and attribution of many outcomes is fraught with methodological difficulties. Nevertheless the output was regarded as reasonably sound due to the fact that:

- Firstly, the research was undertaken by professional economists and the findings were subject to peer review.
- Secondly, a conservative approach was adopted to the estimation of impacts and their valuation in economic terms – for example: general deterrent effects of convictions on other offenders were not assumed; fraud was excluded because of a lack of reliable volume estimates; and potential impacts on persistent and prolific offending were also excluded due to the degree of uncertainty on impact;
- Thirdly, a range of estimates were calculated based on confidence in the underlying data and analysis. Quality scores were used to rate confidence in each estimate as follows:

Confidence & Quality ratings	Key criteria
5	Bottom up estimate; disaggregated to cover the main subtypes; based on a representative sample; based on a large sample; utilizing market prices for benefits.
4	Bottom up estimate; based on a small representative sample; utilizing willingness to pay analysis.
3	Near complete aggregate data triangulated against some bottom up calculations; some disaggregation by main categories.
2	Top down estimate; based on near complete aggregate data; no disaggregation.
1	Top down estimate; many groups/types encompassed by one average; estimates based on small, unrepresentative samples.

Figure 11: Social Value Confidence & Quality ratings

The other key point to note is that the model was dynamic rather than static – the value was updated on a quarterly basis to reflect: changes in the root cause model; programme delivery; updated crime cost and volume data; and research into areas not covered by the original model and to improve the quality of the estimates.

Example 5 – Social Value in the IJIS programme in Queensland, Australia

The Integrated Justice Information Strategy (IJIS) was designed to facilitate inter-agency information sharing and coordination through a combination of improved technology and systems, business process refinement, policy change and legislative amendment. The improved system effectiveness would consequently enhance safety for agency staff, participants and the community. As such it was recognised that the full value from the strategy went beyond direct financial benefits to the government agencies to include benefits to the Queensland community. But the latter were not reflected in the business case and addressing this deficiency was hampered by the absence of a mechanism to quantify the economic and social impacts and no agreement on the indicators that could be used to measure progress

The approach adopted was based on a collaborative partnering arrangement encompassing the main justice agencies (Queensland Police Service, Department of Justice and Attorney General, Queensland Corrective Services, Department of Communities and Department of Child Safety), central agencies (Department of Premier and Cabinet, Queensland Treasury and the Queensland Government Chief Information Office), the IJIS programme team and specialist research consultants.

Key aspects of the methodology adopted were:

1. Desktop research of published data and literature to source and value as many social and economic benefits as possible, including the relevance of particular data sources and literature in the context of their applicability to Queensland.

2. Consultation with all agencies involved with IJIS in order to identify, prioritise and agree on the quantifiable indicators of economic and social benefit. These stakeholders had diverse views, especially in respect of the potential benefits that could be realised from improved information sharing and there was also a concern that the outcomes would be affected by factors beyond the control of the IJIS programme. Following extensive consultation, consensus was reached on the economic and social indica-

72

tors to be used – for example 'increased reporting of crime' was used as a proxy measure for 'improved public confidence'.

3. The mapping of benefit indicators to the criminal justice process, prioritisation of benefit indicator by agency, and the development of a criminal justice sector micro-simulation model to value the nature and extent of the changes as a result of IJIS. The model and input values were validated via workshops with government agency representatives and academics from the Justice Modelling (JMAG) team at Griffith University.

4. The valuation of the social and economic benefits utilised two approaches - the first applied evidence from the research literature and an understanding of the impacts of IJIS sourced via consultation. The second used a computer model to simulate the criminal justice system and outcomes for people of all ages using random simulation.

This analysis also provided the basis for calculating the discounted present value of social benefits and including these benefits in the business case in accordance with Queensland Treasury Benefit-Cost assessment guidelines. The resulting findings demonstrated a sound business investment returning benefits to the criminal justice agencies, central agencies and the community.

[Provided with the kind assistance of Shane Perkins, IJIS, Department of Justice and Attorney General.]

What we see with both the CJS IT and IJIS approaches is the value of a multi-disciplinary approach involving sector specialists and economists. Beyond gaining a more comprehensive view of the potential benefits from the respective investments, an additional form of value came from improved cross agency collaboration in exploring all potential sources of value and the resulting consensus on the appropriate measures to be used. Other areas of commonality include the development of models to quantify the benefits claimed and also to provide a basis for updating them as new information became available.

Chapter 6
Mandatory Projects and Programmes

"It doesn't make sense to treat programs that are legally required the same way as a pure business opportunity. Why attempt to measure benefits for the legally mandated program? The benefit is well known to start with: the company stays in business and the officers stay out of jail!"

John Thorp

Introduction

Some projects and programmes won't necessarily be able to demonstrate a positive financial return on investment. These include those driven by the following investment objectives:

- to meet legal or regulatory requirements – where the investment rationale is the avoidance of the consequences of not complying with the law or regulatory requirements, both financial and non-financial, including damage to organisational reputation;

- the need to maintain business critical operations – and so avoid, or lessen the risk of, the costs of failures in key operational and support systems; and

- in the public sector especially, politically mandated projects, including those designed to avoid, or that are in response to, a major system or policy failure - the investment rationale being to prevent or reduce the likelihood of systemic failures or 'Things Gone Wrong' (TGW's) including failures in the organisation's purpose, core mission or duty of care.

Given the pressing need for some action, many such projects and programmes will proceed, with or without a positive financial return on investment, and this reality needs to be reflected in the investment appraisal criteria and benefits management approaches adopted. So what options are open to us?

Option 1 – Don't expect mandatory projects to demonstrate benefits that exceed the cost.

As with infrastructure investments discussed in the next Chapter, one option is to treat mandatory investments differently from other categories of investment by not expecting them to demonstrate value and excluding them from the benefits management regime. This view is expressed in the quotation from Thorp (2003) at the start of this chapter, and one publication from Gartner (2005) similarly suggests, "*For mandatory projects, focus on measures for meeting requirements on time/on budget.*" But I believe this approach is insufficient because:

- how do you know, <u>really know</u>, that the project will deliver the forecast performance impact in terms of regulatory/legal or policy compliance? Many projects have claimed a "mandatory" justification only for it to become all too clear with hindsight that the project had little chance of actually meeting the original mandate or that it would only partly address that mandate. Conversely, 'must do' projects can also easily become the 'trojan horse' for a whole load of other functionality that would otherwise fail the investment test;

- often the mandate that originally arose in response to a real or perceived threat, no longer applies with the passage of time – and yet the project ploughs on without regularly reaffirming that the mandate is still current; and

- how do you know that the desired impact could not be achieved more cost-effectively?

The latter point is important because as we have said, all investment has an opportunity cost in terms of other investments foregone and unnecessary expenditure in one area means less or delayed expenditure elsewhere. The relevance of this issue to the public sector in particular is illustrated, although in admittedly exaggerated form, by the following from economist Milton Friedman (2004).

Example 6 – Friedman's Four Ways to Spend Money

"*There are four ways in which you can spend money. You can spend your own money on yourself. When you do that, why then you really watch out what you're doing, and you try to get the most for your money. Then you can spend your own money on somebody else. For example, I buy a birthday present for someone. Well, then I'm not so careful about the content of the present, but I'm very careful about the cost. Then, I can spend somebody else's money on myself. And if I spend somebody else's money on myself, then I'm sure going to have a good lunch! Finally, I can spend somebody else's money on somebody else. And if I spend somebody else's money on somebody else, I'm not concerned about how much it is, and I'm not concerned about what I get. And that's government.*"

Sourced from: http://en.wikiquote.org/wiki/Milton_Friedman
1 December 2007.

The point actually applies in the private sector as well – the reality is that in both sectors we are investing, "*other people's money*" whether it be taxpayers' or shareholders' money, and consequently it is incumbent upon us that we really understand and are able to communicate the value we are creating from investment in ICT, and appraise that value in relation to the wider portfolio of potential investments and other potential uses of taxpayers' or shareholders' funds. The same Gartner publication referred to above, also includes the following quote from Ron Puccinelli, Director of IT at the City of Concord, California, "*You should be able to communicate value for all projects, even mandatory ones, by including nonfinancial measures of tangible value.*" But how do we address this?

Option 2 – Justify the investment on the basis of what will happen if you don't invest

For example, in reviewing the case for information sharing initiatives in the criminal justice field in the United States, Michael Geerken (2002) argues that, "*A powerful case for justice system integration is best made by detailing the consequences of a lack of effective electronic data sharing among justice agencies, especially by reference to real-life examples or "horror stories".*"

There is no doubt that such 'horror stories' can provide an extremely effective stimulus to action.

Example 7 - The Bichard Inquiry Report, 22 June 2004

"*On 17 December 2003, Ian Huntley was convicted of the murders of Jessica Chapman and Holly Wells. It is difficult to exaggerate the horror which these murders caused or to begin to imagine the grief of the girls' families....he had been known to the authorities over a period of years. In fact he had come to the attention of Humberside Police in relation to allegations of eight separate sexual offences from 1995 to 1999* (and had been investigated in yet another). This information had not emerged during the vetting check, carried out by Cambridgeshire Constabulary at the time of Huntley's appointment to Soham Village College late in 2001...One of the key failings was the inability of Humberside Police and Social Services to identify Huntley's behaviour pattern soon enough. That was because both viewed each case in isolation and because Social Services failed to share information effectively with the police. It was also because, as the Humberside Chief Constable admitted in his evidence, there were 'systemic and corporate' failures in the way in which Humberside Police managed their intelligence systems....serious delays across police forces in entering data onto the PNC...It is regrettable that so little*

---

progress has been made since 1994 and that, as a result, police forces do not easily or routinely have access to intelligence held about an individual by other police forces."

*four involved allegations of unlawful sexual intercourse with girls under the age of 16 and four involved allegations of rape.

The above case led to a whole raft of initiatives designed to improve the sharing of intelligence between police forces and other parts of the criminal justice system but, no matter how compelling such cases are, justifying an investment on this basis <u>alone</u> is insufficient for several reasons:

- firstly, it means that a major failure is required before action is taken;
- secondly, we are dependent on such failings being at the forefront of decision-makers' attention when the investment case is made, and we are exposed to the risk that failings in another part of the organisation or system may occur and therefore take precedence; and
- thirdly, it can appear to funding bodies that such failures are used by management to justify additional funding and to shift the blame for their occurrence from the service provider to the funding agency.

There is another reason we need to treat this approach with care – and that's because it can be so effective! Kahneman and Tversky (1979) demonstrated that people are generally loss averse i.e. in decision-making we tend to weight losses more than equal gains. Cialdini (2007) similarly argues that people are motivated more by a potential loss than a gain of the same amount, for example, "*homeowners told how much money they could lose from inadequate insulation are more likely to insulate their homes than those told how much money they could save."* Consequently, an investment case framed in terms of what might be lost will tend to be supported more than the same case which is presented in terms of what might be gained – indeed there is some evidence that losses can be twice as painful as gains are pleasurable (Hastie and Dawes, 2001). The issue here is that the underlying business case is unchanged, but the way that it is presented (avoiding a loss as opposed to realising a gain) can significantly affect its chances of being funded. Our best defence against such cognitive biases is to consistently focus on the value created in all cases to ensure projects with the strongest cases are funded. Two approaches that seek to achieve this are outlined below.

Option 3 – The Expected Value approach

This approach calculates the value of the project by estimating its expected value in the following terms:

> Value of a mandatory project = the probability of the undesired event occurring x cost or impact of that event.

According to Curley (2005), Deutsche Bank uses a variation of this approach to value reductions in business risk. The risk of an "event", which is defined as something that could negatively affect the bank, is the product of the probability the event will occur, the likelihood that the bank will be exposed to that event, and the impact of that event. Costs are then estimated both with and without the investment and in this way a value for the reduction in risk can be assessed.

Whilst this appears methodologically sound and intuitively attractive, we are faced with a number of immediate problems:

- How do we assign a value/cost to an uncertain future event? We have already discussed in the last Chapter some of the problems in accurately determining value in the absence of market prices.

- In terms of benefits realisation, we face the problem of how to measure things that don't happen and how to attribute their avoidance to specific initiatives i.e. just because something doesn't happen does not necessarily mean the project was successful – another failing may be just around the corner.

- How do we assess the probability of the event occurring? We can use the past but most publicity material for investment in the stock market includes the disclaimer, "*Past performance is not a guide to future returns*". We also face the problem that future conditions may be different (they usually are) from past conditions and, even putting this aside, what past period do we use to assess the future probabilities (and again, over what period into the future?). Most fundamentally, as we have seen in our consideration of data reliability in Chapter 1, research indicates that even experts suffer from cognitive traps that often limit our ability to make accurate forecasts – as Nobel prize winner Daniel Kahneman (2002) said, "*Remarkably, the intuitive judgments of these experts did not conform to statistical principles with which they were thoroughly familiar.*" In relation to estimates of probability, these cognitive biases include:

- o Most people have an asymmetric attitude to risk, losses are weighted more heavily than gains of a similar amount, and we tend to overreact to small probabilities and under-react to medium and large probabilities;
- o We find it difficult to ignore sunk costs when deciding whether to fund cost escalation – as Piattelli-Palmarini (1994) says, "*once we have actually committed a large sum, we are inclined to add to it more than we would ever have accepted to spend at the beginning*" (which helps explain why killing failing projects is so difficult in practice);
- o Taleb (2004) argues that people are fooled by randomness, "*The brain sees the world as less, far less, random than it actually is*" and rare events are both less rare and less predictable than we think (after the event) that they are. We are also quick to claim personal credit for our successes but equally prone to attribute failures to bad luck (the so-called 'attribution bias')
- o We tend to place too much confidence on results from small samples; and
- o The way events are described and the ease with which they can be recalled (the 'availability' heuristic), affect the probability we assign to them i.e. the more information provided, the greater the probability estimated. Taleb (2004) quotes Tversky and Kahneman who found that both professional predictors and the general public rated a deadly flood caused by an earthquake in California more likely than a fatal flood in the United States (which includes California and floods caused by factors other than earthquakes).

The problem is that many examples in probability appear counter-intuitive - for example, the odds that at least two people in a room of 24 will share the same birthday are better than one in two i.e. you should bet on it – and the odds rise to over 90% when only 36 people are present. Perhaps the best known example illustrating this point is provided by the Monty Hall puzzle which is so counter-intuitive that when Parade magazine printed the problem and the answer in its 'Ask Marilyn' column, around 10,000 readers including mathematicians, wrote to say the answer was wrong!

Example 8 - The Monty Hall Puzzle

You're on a game show and the host shows you three boxes - in each is a slip of paper. The host explains that you will be asked to choose a box and you will win whatever is written on the slip of paper in that box. In two cases the slip of paper is marked "goat" and in the other "car". The

---

host knows what is in each box and says he will invite you to choose a box and will then open one of the other boxes to reveal a slip with 'goat'. You choose your box and the host then indeed opens one of the other two boxes and shows you a slip of paper marked "goat". He then asks whether you want to change your choice to the remaining box or stick with your original choice.

So should you change? Most say it makes no difference as either way you have a 50:50 chance of winning, but the correct answer is 'yes' – and, given that you don't know whether your original choice was for the car or not, always (assuming of course that you prefer a car to a goat). The temptation is to assume that as there are two boxes left the chance that the slip of paper with "car" is in either box is equal. But this is not the case. Consider the probabilities associated with your original choices:

- You chose the box with the car - the probability that your original choice was the box with the car is one in three. In this case your best course of action is to stick with your original choice.
- You chose one of the two boxes with a goat - the probability that you chose a goat at the start was 2 in 3 and the fact that the host has opened a box to reveal a slip of paper with "goat" means that the car must be in the other box – in which case you are best off changing your choice.

So in 1 case out of three you should stick and in 2 out of 3 you should change. The trouble is you don't know what you've chosen and therefore you should change your choice and in so doing you double the probability that you will win the car. If this seems odd – re-read the above!

What this all means is that the Expected Value approach has serious methodological issues associated with it. Fortunately there is another approach that provides a way through the impasse, and which accepts the reality of mandated or non-discretionary projects, whilst also maintaining a focus on capturing value.

Option 4 Making implicit assumptions explicit – the 'Willingness to Pay' approach

There is an implicit assumption that the value of compliance with laws and regulations and avoidance of a policy failure represents, at a minimum, the net cost of the project – if not we would not invest. We can take this a step further by making this implicit cost explicit, based on a 'willingness to pay' approach i.e. requiring the Investment Committee, and in the public sector Senior Management and even Ministers, to formally agree that the cost of the programme or project, net of any direct benefits, represents the value that they place on compliance or the avoidance of 'Things Gone Wrong'. But this is more than a shifty piece of 'benefits spin' designed to re-categorise cost as value – the decision to invest is also dependent on three pieces of supporting analysis:

- Firstly, a detailed cause and effect analysis (benefits map or model) to demonstrate the rationale for linking the project to the business requirement (approved by the Senior Business Sponsor) along with an assessment of the degree of confidence we have that the project will address the issue at hand effectively i.e. what is the evidence base on which a cause and effect linkage is premised? This is of course not-withstanding the problems cited above in terms of reliably assigning probabilities and determining cause and effect. Accepting these issues, it is judged preferable that we attempt to understand the logic on which our investment decisions are based and the confidence that we have in the claims made.

- Secondly, the measures and indicators (both in terms of final outcomes and 'leading' indicators) that will be used to assess project success and impact need to be identified; and

- Thirdly, an options analysis demonstrating that the net cost represents the most cost-effective solution to the issue (approved by the Finance Director).

An example of this approach is provided in the case study below.

Example 9 – Political Mandate: The Violent & Sex Offender Register (ViSOR) project

The Criminal Justice and Court Services Act of 2000, consolidated by the Criminal Justice Act of 2003, places duties on the police, probation and prisons to make arrangements for the identification, risk assessment and management of violent and sexual offenders in the community, known as MAPPA - the Multi-Agency Public Protection Arrangements (MAPPA) process.

These provisions require close working between prisons, probation and police, and an integrated approach to the management of sexual, violent

---

and other dangerous offenders. These arrangements were based on manual processes with consequent delays in information sharing. This project sought to provide a secure database that could be accessed by the Police, Probation and Prison Services enabling the timely sharing of intelligence, risk assessment and risk management information on individual violent and sex offenders. This was also forecast to improve offender management and supervision and so enhance both staff and public protection.

As with many such projects, it was unable to demonstrate a positive financial return on investment – how do we put a price on the more timely provision of such information? This could have been addressed by using a major failure to make the case for investment or by estimating the costs associated with failings that could have been prevented by effective information sharing and the probability of those failings re-occurring. In practice the deficiencies with these approaches were recognised and the Senior Responsible Officer (SRO) sponsored analysis to: articulate the value proposition via a Benefits Dependency Network (BDN); to agree the success indicators; and demonstrate cost-effectiveness. This analysis provided a basis for Ministerial agreement to invest on the basis that the cost required represented a fair price to pay to gain the qualitative and quantitative benefits identified from improved information sharing.

The advantages of the 'willingness to pay' approach are that it is based on making implicit judgments explicit, specifically articulating the real justification for the project and, as always, being clear about the benefits that we are buying.

Chapter 7
Infrastructure Investments

"When you don't invest in infrastructure, you are going to pay sooner or later"

Mike Parker

Introduction

Investments in infrastructure provide the foundation for organisational performance by maintaining and improving current services (in terms of reliability and security) and providing the platform for expansion to meet additional demands, both in respect of current services and new services (both planned and unplanned). The specific problem we face is that the value from investing in infrastructure is not always immediately obvious. Indeed some have argued that investment in infrastructure is the 'cost of doing business'. Gartner (2005) for example, reports that, *"Several CIO interviewees said that their business executives treat infrastructure investments as a "tax", and as long as the business doesn't experience a problem, and the investment stays within benchmarked boundaries, there is little focus on benefits."*

The result is that such investments are not exposed to the usual investment appraisal and benefits management regimes. The trouble with this approach is that, firstly, it ignores the fact that all investments imply choice in relation to timing and with regard to the opportunity costs associated with other potential investments foregone. Without some appraisal of value for money how are we to decide how much to spend on infrastructure, on what aspects of our infrastructure we should invest, and when? Secondly, treating infrastructure investments in this way fails to recognise that in many cases, the value implicit in infrastructure investments is a <u>potential</u> value and this value will only be realised if the investment is exploited through usage (much akin to financial options where value is only realised if the option is exercised) – and if this value is not managed there is a risk that it won't be realised. It's too easy in practice to treat previous investments as sunk costs and so to fail to exploit the capability that has been created. The relevance of this has been highlighted by Tallon and Kraemer (2003) who propose a two way relationship between IT investment and business strategy i.e. investment in IT should support the business strategy (although with sufficient flexibility to respond to shifts in business strategy) and the business strategy also needs to capitalise on the capability created. Crucial in this regard is effective engagement between business and IT – something we shall return to in Chapter 9.

A slight improvement over the 'tax on the business' approach is to benchmark infrastructure spend. But once again there are some fairly obvious issues with this approach: the benchmark organisations may not be comparable; the services provided may not be comparable; who decides whether the benchmark organisations represent best practice; and are the levels of spend appropriate given the business strategy? Additionally the focus is on minimising cost rather than optimising benefits. Benchmarking can provide a useful source of data that prompts further investigation, but it does not provide a definitive measure of relative or absolute value.

For these reasons, excluding infrastructure investments from the benefits management regime is regarded as being insufficient. But we face an immediate problem – as Gartner reports (2004), "*infrastructure business cases are particularly difficult for two reasons: The benefits are not always obvious to the end user or business leadership, and they are spread across multiple parties...In fact, many benefits of an infrastructure initiative are like an insurance policy – you only notice them when things go wrong.*"

The challenge we therefore face is how to articulate this value and manage its realisation in a meaningful manner? We outline below an approach that takes a holistic approach to capturing infrastructure benefits and which focuses on managing the exploitation of this value on an active basis. But first, what do we mean by infrastructure investments and what benefits do such investments provide?

Definitions – infrastructure and its benefits

IT infrastructure will include different elements in different organisations – for example, operating systems, servers, storage, desktops, disaster recovery, security and networks are commonly recognised as infrastructure, but it may also include help desks, e-mail and office automation software. Infrastructure is therefore an amalgam of investments in hardware, software, processes and people. While definitions will vary between organisations, what is more important for our purposes, is to note that the full value inherent in an infrastructure investment depends on other investments which it supports i.e. whilst there may be some direct benefits (cost savings for example) many of the benefits are enabling rather than direct in nature. These benefits include:

1. Cost savings – where for example, up-front investment in more modern infrastructure and rationalisation of infrastructure provision improves efficiency and/or reduces running costs across the organisation.

2. Cost avoidance – i.e. the savings from the avoidance of systems failures. These include both financial and non-financial costs arising from, for example, a security failure and include the costs of reputational damage. Such costs are most commonly associated with the private sector where loss of reputation can have immediate bottom line effects, but they also apply in the public sector in the context of Mark Moore's concept of trust as an aspect of Public Value as discussed in Chapter 5.

3. Improved operational support – where more modern infrastructure provides greater service reliability, faster response times etc.

4. The flexibility to accommodate:

   ▪ planned and unplanned expansions in demand associated with current applications;
   ▪ planned and unplanned expansions in demand associated with new applications; and
   ▪ organisational re-structuring associated with, for example, machinery of government changes in the public sector, and merger and acquisitions in the private sector.

As will become clear, I advocate an approach that includes consideration of all four forms of value.

Approaches to capturing infrastructure benefits

One common approach is to recharge the cost of the infrastructure to the applications that use the infrastructure. This has immediate attractions because it relates the costs of the infrastructure to the known applications that it will support. But this can only be applied to current and planned applications, and there may be limited incentives to manage costs down. In practice infrastructure supports not only existing and planned requirements, but also uncertain future applications and demand. Failure to recognise the value of this flexibility to meet unknown future demands can be damaging to organisational health and lead to increased costs in the longer term. A report from Booz Allen Hamilton (2002) for example, comments that, "*Early investments in e-services are burdened with the costs associated with building required infrastructure and skills. Cost analyses that do not incorporate foundational value can make calculating and demonstrating a short-term or even long-term value difficult or even impossible. Decisions made based on these calculations will stifle innovation and make progress toward transforming government sluggish at best."*

A holistic approach is therefore recommended, that incorporates all forms of value - cost savings and costs avoided (particularly relevant with regard to replacement infrastructure), improved operational support, and the flexibility to respond to shifts in demand. With regard to the last point – this is no academic argument as Ashby's Law of Requisite Variety suggests that, *"the element in the system which has the most flexibility is the element that controls the system."* So the ability to respond to unanticipated changes has a value – and indeed the research by Tallon and Kraemer (2003) referred to above, found what they refer to as, *"an alignment paradox"* – strategic alignment can lead to increased value from IT but this only holds to a certain point beyond which payoff falls and this is, at least in part, due to the need to maintain a degree of flexibility in both business and IT strategy. But this does not mean that we can just assign a 'value of flexibility' badge to any cost-benefit shortfall and use that to justify increased spend on infrastructure. As I argue throughout this book, all projects should be seen as investments and that means they need to demonstrate a return (however that is measured) that justifies the costs. So how do we achieve this with regard to investments in infrastructure?

A first step is to set the investment in infrastructure in the strategic context – via Strategic Contribution Analysis (see Chapter 3) to identify the infrastructure investments, and the applications that will run on that infrastructure, and the contribution that they will make to the business strategy (more on this below); and by allocating a segment in the change portfolio to infrastructure investments and managing these investments over a multi-year planning horizon. Peter Weill of the Massachusetts Institute of Technology, argues that IT investment should be managed as a portfolio with four asset classes, each with their own investment objectives and hence different investment criteria will apply to each – see Figure 12 sourced from Weill & Aral (2004) and Weill & Johnson (2005).

As with financial portfolio management, the IT portfolio needs to be balanced across the four asset classes or segments, to ensure alignment with business strategy in both the short and long term. Analysis of IT spend in this manner enables consideration as to whether resources are appropriately distributed across the segments in the context of environmental conditions and business priorities.

Asset Class	Description	Investment Objective	Av. Weighted investment in 2005
Strategic	Applications to support entry into a new market, development of new or customized products etc.	To gain competitive advantage or position in the market place.	11%
Informational	Applications providing information to manage, account, control, plan, comply, report, communicate with customers.	To provide more and better information for any purpose including to account, manage, control, report, communicate, collaborate or analyse.	17%
Transactional	Applications to automate repetitive transactions, cut costs, increase throughput.	To cut costs or increase throughput so reducing unit costs and increasing productivity.	26%
Infrastructure	Shared IT services such as the network, customer databases, pc/laptops, help desk, data centre, servers, security, middleware but not applications.	Base foundation of shared IT services used by multiple applications. Such investments can be to reduce cost via standardisation or consolidation and/or to provide a flexible platform for future business initiatives.	46%

Figure 12: Peter Weill's Four Asset Classes

Gartner's Light et al (2005) offer a similar analysis with 'infrastructure', 'utility' (mission critical but not performance improving), 'business enhancement' and 'frontier' (high return, high risk) categories. A survey of 500 clients found the average breakdown of spend to be: 47% on infrastructure and 53% on applications analysed as: 21% on utility, 21% on enhancement and 11% on frontier. Interestingly, the Government analysis showed a higher commitment than in the private sector to the 'infrastructure' and 'utility' categories, in which cost reduction rather than business value enhancement is the aim:

	Frontier	Enhancement	Utility	Infrastructure
Federal	13%	22%	22%	44%
Local	3%	12%	30%	55%
State	5%	12%	24%	58%
All	6%	14%	26%	54%

Figure 13: Gartner's Four Asset Class approach to IT portfolio segmentation

The value of such analyses is that they enable comparisons against plan, other organisations, and over time, as well as being used to target reductions in infrastructure and utility spend so releasing resources for business value adding applications.

So a first step in managing infrastructure value is to examine the proportion of the portfolio spend on infrastructure over time (to assess cost efficiency of infrastructure spend) and in relation to the business strategy (to assess the cost effectiveness of that infrastructure spend).

The next step is to take into consideration the value of applications (both planned and potential) that will run on that infrastructure. One approach is to borrow from the financial sector and apply options theory to the project and programme environment i.e. the use of real options theory. This is appealing because investments in infrastructure have some similarities with financial options in that their value is dependent on the outcome of uncertain future events. The problem is that whilst in financial markets there is a multitude of quantitative data that underpins the inputs into the Black-Scholes formula that is used to value a 'call' (the right to buy a share at a stipulated price) and a 'put' (the right to sell a share at a stipulated price), in the project and programme environment the input factors are far less certain – as Yu has said, "*reliable data for estimating...are generally lacking.*". An added problem concerns the difficulty many managers face in understanding the approach. As a result, whilst the use of real options theory has theoretical attractions, there are real impediments to its use in many real-life situations.

An alternative is to use a methodology that starts with the relatively easy to assess cost savings and costs avoided and then uses the organisation's strategic plans, environmental scanning and portfolio planning processes to identify planned and potential applications that may exploit the investment in infrastructure. This provides a basis for capturing all forms of value created including flexibility – or the potential opportunity value inherent in the investment in infrastructure. The added advantage is that this approach also provides a mechanism for managing the realisation of this value on an active basis going forward. The four stage process is as follows:

1. The first stage is to identify the pipeline of opportunities, planned and potential, that will exploit or leverage the capability and capacity created by the investment in infrastructure. Key sources for this will be the organisation's strategic plan and environmental scanning process as well as the IT strategy and application roadmap or project pipeline. These sources should be reviewed to identify relevant projects and initiatives.

2. Stage 2 values these opportunities. Costs and benefits should be prudent and should therefore be adjusted for optimism bias as discussed in Chapter 1. If the project has advanced as far as Outline Business Case Stage this may be achieved by applying empirically derived adjustments to the costs and benefits or reference class forecasting, potentially augmented by use of the PERT estimating formula:

   [Optimistic Cost/Benefit profile + Pessimistic Cost/Benefit profile + (4 x Most Likely Cost/Benefit profile)] divided by 6.

   The input data can be derived by using the initial cost estimate (adjusted for optimism bias or itself derived from the cost/benefits of completed reference class projects) as a "Most Likely" estimate and then performing sensitivity analysis on the key cost and benefits drivers to develop an optimistic and pessimistic cost/benefit estimate reflecting local circumstances.

   We can't count all this potential value because there is no guarantee that all the potential projects will come to fruition – we therefore need to adjust the values for the probability that each of the individual projects will be progressed. We have already discussed the problems inherent in estimating reliable probabilities although these can be overcome, at least in part, by validating the results with an independent Investment Committee, Portfolio Unit or Value Management Office, and by using a standard set of criteria for assessing probability. The Criminal Justice IT programme for example assessed the probability of potential projects becoming 'live' using a weighted scorecard incorporating consideration of factors such as: scale of strategic contribution; whether the project was designed to meet a legislative or regulatory requirement; whether funding was already in place; the scale of stakeholder commitment; relative attractiveness; and relative achievability. In this way, the forecast value of each opportunity is adjusted for the probability that it will come to fruition. When totalled, these individual values provide a value for the project pipeline as a whole.

3. At Stage 3, the probability adjusted potential value of the project pipeline calculated above will need to be adjusted for:

    - known constraints - for example, technical constraints (the capacity of the infrastructure to support the potential demands on it); funding constraints that mean attractive opportunities need to be sequenced; and whether the business can accommodate the scale of business change implied; and
    - synergies – the ability to re-use solutions, tools, methodologies and capabilities.

4. Stage 4 - the output of Stages 1-3 will be a value for the infrastructure investment that incorporates known cost savings and costs avoided as well as a probability-adjusted value of planned and potential applications. But we don't need to stop there – the 'added value' from this 'potential opportunity value' process is that on a periodic basis (say six monthly or annually) we can update the value to reflect changes in the project pipeline and benefits realisation and so validate the value claimed. This is achieved by monitoring of two key metrics:

    - Opportunity Conversion – the number of projects that move from opportunity to live project status; and
    - Benefit Conversion – the comparison of benefits realised (net of cost) against original forecast net benefits.

The advantages of the 'Potential Opportunity Value' approach are that it incorporates known cost savings and cost avoidance benefits as well as the value of flexibility i.e. the value of potential applications that are dependent on that infrastructure. Equally importantly, the approach provides a basis for on-going active management of the exploitation of this investment – in terms of launching projects and realising benefits. It is this aspect of active management to create value that we address in the next Section.

Section 2. Summary

We've seen that it is important that we capture all forms of value: to ensure that we are investing limited funds cost-effectively; for accountability reasons; and because it lays the basis for benefits realisation. This means that in addition to the efficiency and effectiveness benefits discussed in Section 1, we also need to identify, quantify and if necessary, value:

1. Cross departmental benefits – agreement with the recipients here is particularly important. Cross-departmental working groups can play a key role in ensuring systems are exploited to their full potential beyond the sponsoring organisation.

2. Citizen benefits and wider social value – multi-criteria analysis and research into the drivers of customer satisfaction can be used to identify and quantify these benefits. Valuing them in the absence of market prices is problematic, although contingent valuation techniques and econometric models can be used to complete a comprehensive benefit proposition.

3. The benefits from mandatory projects using a 'willingness to pay' appraisal based on detailed cause and effect modelling, clarity on the success measures, and confirmation that the performance impact or risk reduction cannot be achieved more cost-effectively.

4. Infrastructure projects – capturing benefits in terms of cost savings, costs avoided, business continuity, and supporting both planned and unplanned applications using a potential opportunity value approach.

As we say above, this in turn lays the basis for benefits realisation and value creation and it is to these subjects that we now turn.

Section 3
Realising Benefits and Creating Value

"Price is what you pay. Value is what you get."

Warren Buffett

After reading this Section you will understand how we can:

- Manage the benefits realisation process to ensure benefits are realised in practice. This includes:

    o managing benefits in the context of the wider change portfolio and regularly re-confirming the benefits case still holds true;
    o booking benefits wherever possible; and
    o also tracking benefits against forecast.

- Move beyond tracking forecast benefits to value creation by managing benefits from an organisational perspective and establishing a forward looking focus, based on learning and continuous participative engagement between the IT function, project teams and system users.

So far we have laid the basis for benefits realisation by capturing all forms of value whilst also ensuring that those claims are as robust as possible. We now need to consider how we manage the actual realisation of benefits in practice and that's the subject of this section.

If we lived in a world without change, populated by rational economic man that would be that – we'd track benefits realisation against plan and where negative variations occurred, we'd pull out the economist's toolkit of incentives and sanctions to restore the system to equilibrium. But the world's not like that. Firstly, things change – as Harold Macmillan said when asked what can most easily steer a government off course, *"Events, dear boy. Events"*. Secondly, the world is not inhabited by people that behave as economists often assume. John Seddon (2007) quotes Adam Curtis's TV series 'The Trap' – *"only two groups in society actually behave in a rational self-interested way in all experimental situations. One is economists themselves, the other is psychopaths."* People are motivated by factors other than the 'carrot' of financial rewards and the 'stick' of the consequences of failure – and we need to tap into these other factors if we are to realise the full benefits from our investments. Thirdly, benefits are realised from the combination of technology, process change and people actually using the system. They are consequently in many cases 'emergent' i.e. benefits emerge as the users use the information provided and find ways in which they can exploit the capability and capacity created.

This means that as Farbey, Land and Targett (1999) suggest, evaluation, "*is always taking place on a moving staircase.*" This in turn requires that our benefits management process needs to look forward rather than back, and we need to actively engage with users throughout the project life cycle in a continuous and shared exploration of how value can be created. In short, we can win hearts as well as minds by creating what Peter Senge (1999) referred to as, "*a shared picture of the future we seek to create*". We explore how this can be achieved and how we can go beyond benefits realisation to value creation in Chapter 9 – although as we shall see the benefits realisation process should not be the passive process suggested above. Managed with a bias for action, it can also be part of the value creation process.

Chapter 8
Realising the Benefits –
Tracking and Reporting

*"When you can measure what you are speaking about, and ex-
press it in numbers, you know something about it; but when you
cannot measure it, when you cannot express it in numbers, your
knowledge is of a meager and unsatisfactory kind".*

William Thomson later Lord Kelvin

Introduction

Having captured all potential forms of value in our benefits forecasts and
ensured that these forecasts are robust and realisable, our objective now
is to ensure that the performance matches the promise i.e. to ensure that
forecast benefits are realised in practice. Our coverage of this subject
starts with consideration of the question, '*Why measure*?'. We then challenge the '*forget the business case once funding is awarded and consider
benefits once the system is implemented*' paradigm. Instead, it is argued
that benefits realisation requires that we re-visit the benefits case on a
regular basis and consider it in the wider context of the organisation's
business priorities and its change portfolio. We then move on to consider
tracking and reporting progress – not just as an accountability mechanism, but more significantly as part of the information feedback loop in
which learning leads to action and value creation. We conclude with
some thoughts on the aspect of selecting appropriate measures of benefits realisation.

Why measure?

A question that is often posed is why measure? This view is summed up
by the Chinese proverb, "*You don't fatten a pig by weighing it*". From this
perspective, measurement is a backward looking activity that is an unnecessary non-value-adding activity. The opposite view is summed up by
the management adage, "*You can't manage what you don't measure*"
and the Cabinet Office (2002) states, "*It is only possible to be sure that
change has worked if we can measure the delivery of the benefits it is
supposed to bring.*" So whilst weighing the pig may not fatten it, it does
provide feedback that can be used to assess whether the pig is gaining
weight and whether any additional action (feeding in this case) is required.

Measuring benefits realisation is important for several other reasons:

- to act as a counter to the tendency to over-estimate benefits in the business case. If the business case writer and project sponsor know that benefits claimed will be tracked and they will be held to account for their realisation, they are more likely to ensure that benefits claimed are reasonable and that appropriate plans are put in place for their realisation. This also helps build confidence on the part of stakeholders particularly those involved in the funding allocation process;

- for accountability purposes i.e. to demonstrate that what was forecast has been delivered;

- it helps communicate that senior management takes benefits realisation seriously and identifies the areas that management should focus on – as reflected in the saying, "*what gets measured gets done*";

- to ensure that the full potential value of the investment is realised – tracking benefits helps identify areas where action is required to address benefits shortfalls or to exploit unanticipated benefits; and

- to provide learning on 'what works' and to inform future investment decisions and the benefit management process – not least by providing an empirical dataset that can be used to inform the preparation and appraisal of future estimates of benefits.

From this perspective benefits measurement rather than being a passive, backward-looking activity, focusing on evaluation of performance against target, is rather an active, forward looking, value-adding activity – and one that can actually drive increased benefits realisation and value creation by providing management information that enables both corrective action and exploitation of benefits that were not forecast at the planning stage. This issue is re-visited in the next Chapter.

Regular re-assessment of, and re-commitment to, the benefits case

The traditional approach to benefits management calls for a business case that is regularly updated throughout the project life cycle. In practice this rarely happens. Instead the business case is prepared to obtain funding for the desired option. The case is then largely forgotten as the emphasis switches to development and implementation, only for it to be re-visited if, for some unfortunate reason it is required, for example, by a gate review. By the time someone asks whether the forecast benefits have been realised, those that made the original decision to invest are usually long gone and the investment has been made – so consequently, if the benefits can't be demonstrated there seems little point in spending more money trying to justify expenditure that is any case sunk.

But it does not need to be so – applying a project portfolio management approach can help ensure that the benefits case remains sound and that management commitment and accountability is maintained throughout the project life cycle. This involves five stages.

1. <u>Dividing the organisation's ICT project portfolio into segments</u> as discussed in Chapter 7. The investment criteria used should be tailored to the investment objectives of each segment:

   - *Business applications* – Cost-benefit appraisal, with the benefits including financial benefits, contribution to business priorities and strategic targets, measured using net present value and Strategic Contribution Analysis as discussed in Chapter 3.
   - *New infrastructure* – Potential Opportunity Value/Foundation Value as discussed in Chapter 7.
   - *Replacement infrastructure* – cost saving over the current systems.
   - *Mandatory projects* – lowest net present cost on a 'willingness to pay' basis, subject to confirmation that the project will meet the compliance requirements and cannot be achieved more cost-effectively (see Chapter 6).

2. <u>Reviewing the benefits case in the context of the wider business change project portfolio</u>. Whilst the benefits may look reasonable when a project business case is appraised, we also need to examine it in relation to other projects and programmes within the project portfolio for:

   - Any dependencies between projects which could impact on benefits realisation;
   - The impact of any constraints such as the availability of skilled project managers, programmers, system architects etc; and
   - The accumulated business change – is it achievable? Consideration should be given to the scale, timing and scope of the change i.e. how many people are affected and does the change relate to the task, the skills required, or does it also imply attitudinal change?

3. <u>Project stage or phase gates</u> i.e. project funding is not a once and for all decision. Funding should be provided to take a project to the next gate review at which time the benefits justification should be re-visited and re-confirmed in the context of project performance, changes in organisational priorities and the environment. These gate reviews can be organised around relevant project phases (e.g. Scoping, Development, Testing, and Implementation) or for example, around the main business case approval stages i.e. Feasibility Study/Concept Case, Strategic Outline Business Case, Outline Business Case, and Full Business Case. Whichever model is adopted, the gate review should represent a re-appraisal of the case and should encompass:

- Consideration as to whether the benefits are still robust and realisable and justify the continued investment;
- Formal re-commitment to benefits realisation by the senior business sponsor and the recipients. In this way there is no '*that was agreed by the predecessor's predecessor'* claims – accountability is therefore something that happens throughout the project life cycle rather than being an ex-ante process alone.

Where the benefits case no longer stacks up the bullet needs to be bitten – as the KPMG Global IT Project Management Survey in 2005 said, *"cancelling a project unlikely to deliver expected benefits should not be seen as a failure – failing to cancel such a project should be."*

Example 10 - Re-appraisal of the Benefits Case: the Victorian Investment Management Standard

The Victorian Government's Investment Logic Map was referred to when we considered benefits modelling in Chapter 3. The workshops that are used to determine the problem, solution and benefits definitions are however not one off events. Instead they are repeated at specified intervals to test whether the investment logic still holds. The result is a re-commitment to the Benefits Realisation Plan and hence increased confidence in benefits realisation.

---

4. <u>Regular portfolio level reviews.</u> Whilst stage gates occur at the project level, there should also be regular portfolio level reviews every quarter, six months or at least annually. The objectives of these reviews are to assess portfolio performance, the continued balance of

the organisation's project portfolio, and to ensure that the allocation of resources continues to represent the optimum return from available funds. From a benefits perspective they include:

- At project level - confirmation that the project Benefits Profiles and Benefits Realisation Plans are up to date and remain achievable;
- At portfolio level - review of benefits realisation across the portfolio: are we ahead of plan and what lessons have been learned?

The corollary of this active approach to managing investments 'in flight' is that we need to really take to heart Number 7 in the NAO/OGC's Common causes of project failure – *"Too little attention to breaking development and implementation into manageable steps."* If we don't do this, killing failing or non-strategically aligned projects and re-allocating funding between projects and programmes, will be more difficult and more expensive. A modular approach to project design and delivery therefore ensures that at least some benefits are realised and at the same time, it also facilitates active management of the organisation's project portfolio.

5. <u>Formative Post-Implementation Review (PIR) or evaluation</u>. Review of projects post-implementation is one of those activities that everyone knows "should" be done, but what's the point – the investment has been made, the project team has disbanded and the SRO has probably moved on to another high ranking job. The result is that where such reviews are undertaken they are often more form than substance with little effective action being taken. Ward (2006) for example, notes that in one European (including the UK) survey, *"80% report that the review and evaluation of completed projects is also inadequate"*. This attitude betrays a misunderstanding about the real purpose or potential value of the PIR – the focus should be less on 'how did we perform compared to a long distant forecast', and more on, 'what did we learn and how can we exploit this learning to derive value not just from this specific project, but also from other projects'? A particular focus should be on capturing emergent benefits (i.e. those that were not anticipated at the time of the original business case and benefits realisation plan) and disseminating them to other users. This forward looking focus was adopted by the WUYJ programme as illustrated in Example 11.

Example 11 – Post Implementation Review on the WUYJ Programme: a 'learning experience'

Within the Wiring Up Youth Justice (WUYJ) Programme, the purpose of Post Implementations Reviews is threefold and addresses the following broad questions:

How successful was the implementation? This question seeks to understand how well the implementation was conducted, with a view to improving implementation not just on that specific project, but also on other projects within the Programme.
What has changed? This question allows for continual validation of benefits via evaluating behavioural change as the driver for benefits realisation.
What actions are required to embed behavioural change and to ensure benefits continue to be realised? The goal here is to encourage local ownership of the benefits realisation process

[Provided with the kind agreement of Paul Griffiths, WUYJ Programme, Business Change Coordinator and Lisa Stewart, WUYJ Benefits Manager.]

Benefits forecasting is therefore not a one-off activity – rather it is something that should be re-visited on a regular basis and be accompanied by formal re-commitment to the benefits case and to their realisation in practice at both project gate and portfolio level reviews.

Benefits tracking and reporting

As we said at the start of this chapter, the objective of tracking realisation is to ensure that the promise matches the performance. Jeffery Kaplan (2005) argues, "*A lot of people ask how to track the results of IT and project investments. Don't track them. Book them! Build the expected benefits into the financial forecast or resource plan.*"

'Booking' benefits does have a number of advantages – firstly, we gain greater confidence that benefits will be realised. Secondly, there is greater clarity about the benefits that will be realised, and thirdly, it provides a basis for engaging the user in planning how benefits will be realised (so long as those benefits are realistic). Wherever possible benefits should therefore be booked in:

- departmental budgets, unit costs, headcount targets and efficiency plans in the case of efficiency benefits;

- strategic and delivery plans in the case of effectiveness benefits;

- personal performance targets – with some scope for determining how the benefits are realised being left to the individual. The OGC's 'Managing Successful Programmes' says, "*One way to make this 'ownership' meaningful is to link benefits realisation to personal performance targets.*"

But as discussed in Chapter 3, we need to check that these benefits are realised in practice – for example we can take funding out of a budget but if the efficiencies are not realised we will only impact on output or service quality. Similarly we can book benefits in unit performance targets – but we need to track that performance and have some assurance that the benefits from the project have contributed to any identified performance improvement. What should therefore be clear is that we cannot escape the need to track and report on benefits, but this does not have to be a major new bureaucracy if we:

- use the existing performance management system wherever possible and relate benefits to organisational measures of success via Strategic Contribution Analysis as discussed in Chapter 3. Where this is not practical, sampling techniques should be employed rather than blanket measurements;

- apply the Exception Principle – focusing management attention on the areas where action is required. A Value Management Office can play a key role in not only compiling progress reports, but also analysing them and alerting management to areas where action is required – both in terms of bringing realisation back onto track and in terms of leveraging learnings to realise additional benefits;

- ensure the tracking effort is commensurate with the benefits to be realised and by applying the 80:20 rule to focus on the most material benefits. The approach adopted in the CJS IT portfolio was for example, to identify the top ten benefits of each project and to summarise the key information from the benefits profiles and Benefits Realisation Plan onto a single page report. Progress was then tracked and reported on a quarterly basis using a report that included:

  o brief descriptions of the benefits, their categories, economic value and performance impact, trajectory, who was responsible for benefits realisation and the measures or indicators used to track realisation;

o RAG assessments of progress against plan/forecast for each of the major benefits;

o an assessment of benefits management maturity with RAG (Red, Amber, Green) assessments for: Quality of the benefits forecast; Scale of benefits forecast; Quality of benefits planning; and Likelihood of benefits realisation; and

o approval by the project's Senior Responsible Officer.

There's one point that should be made to those that see this as an additional form of bureaucracy – they presumably accept that costs need to be managed with a dedicated finance function, financial and management accounting systems with charts of account, data capture systems and regular budgetary reports? Well let's not forget the objective of investing in ICT projects and programmes is to realise benefits. We therefore should not be ashamed to argue that these benefits should be managed at least as robustly as project cost.

Consideration will also need to be given to the question of how long benefits should be tracked and measured. A red flag that indicates an organisation is on the wrong path is when people ask, "*how long do we have to track benefits for?*" This indicates the focus is on tracking against forecast rather than trying to understand how value is being created. The answer in practice is that no hard and fast answer can be given that will apply to all circumstances, but in general, tracking and measurement should continue until benefits have been realised and the value to be derived from tracking no longer outweighs the implied costs of measurement.

We also need to remember that the objective is not to measure benefits for the sake of it, but to ensure they are realised. Management's job is not to make the inevitable happen – and even if no action is taken this should be a result of a deliberate decision on management's behalf. Tracking benefits realisation is therefore an active not a passive process, but what is crucial is that we have meaningful and reliable benefits measures. We have already touched on some of the potential problems in relation to long time spans between initiative and outcomes and the issue of attributing outcomes to individual initiatives. Three techniques can help address this. Firstly, as we discussed in Chapter 3, a benefits measurement taxonomy can provide a suite of metrics (quantitative financial or economic, quantitative non-financial and qualitative) that relate to the underlying benefit that is being measured. Secondly, a combination of outcome measures and lead or proxy indicators may be used, particularly where there is an extended cause and effect chain. Thirdly, ICT systems will only have the desired performance impacts if the information is used effectively by the users. Consequently appropriate measures and indicators of usage need to be developed and used.

A further point to bear in mind is that measures are not without effect – on the one hand, the Hawthorne experiments showed that the act of measurement can influence what is being measured in a positive manner. On the other hand measurement can have unintended consequences of the negative kind where changes in the indicator are pursued at the expense of overall system performance and people engage in gaming behaviour and appearance manipulation. Seddon (2008) argues that such behaviour is, "*ubiquitous and systematic*" as, "*Targets drive people to use their ingenuity to meet the target, not improve performance.*" According to Bottoms and Wiles (1996), "*the attention of members of organisations can sometimes be focused on presentation of the best available data for the purpose of performance indicators, rather than upon the deeper underlying purposes of the activities in question.*" The answer is to adopt a forward-facing perspective that focuses on organisational learning as a basis for value creation, rather than a backward-looking tracking approach that is fixated on comparing actuals against forecast. The ethos should thus be one of planning for success rather than attributing blame, and should be based on close engagement with users to identify measures that are meaningful to them, and employing multiple measures and indicators to provide different perspectives on performance.

Ultimately it's a case of, in the words of the song by Melvin 'Sy' Oliver and James 'Trummy' Young, "*T'ain't What You Do (It's the Way That You Do It)*". If measures are chosen by considering what influences the user and are used to inform understanding rather than to punish, the result rather than appearance manipulation can be value creation. Recent Cabinet Office guidance on promoting customer satisfaction (2008) quotes Tony Hinkley of Dudley Council as saying, "*Feedback provides insight whereas targets distort actions.*" The following examples neatly demonstrate the point.

Example 12 – Measures that engage

"*When working with a crisp factory in the North East of England we noticed the production line waste figures were represented using graphs showing % good product produced by shift by line proudly pinned up on the notice board at the end of each production line. The performance had hovered between 98.0 and 98.5% good production for the past few*

---

months. I asked a line operator what these figures actually meant. She said she did not really know as she never really got to grips with percentages at school but it was clear to her that 98.5% good production was better than 98%. We watched the line manager dutifully post the figures for yesterday at the start of each shift on the notice board and watched the operators never give them a second glance. This was a classic habitual ritual that you can see being acted out up and down the country in any production area or indeed most offices each week.

We tackled this by getting the performance measures to actually mean something to the target audience they were aimed at – the crisp line operators. We first discovered what they cared about and found along with many hailing from the Geordie nation they were all passionate members of the 'Toon Army' – (this means they support Newcastle United football club). We calculated how many bags of crisps 1.5 – 2% production waste actually amounted to (a very large number indeed) and then got a seating plan for Sunderland's football stadium (Newcastle's fiercest rivals). We changed the measure to represent how many Sunderland supporters we could supply with free bags of crisps each week if we continued at current performance levels. We represented this by shading in the number of seats awarded a free bag of crisps in the Sunderland stadium graphic.

This sparked the operators imagination and in no time at all production lines were operating at 99.5% good production on the basis that 'the crisps we make are simply too good for the poor Mackems' (the derogative name Geordies give to their North East neighbours). Now in consultancy and scientific parlance this is known as the Hawthorne effect - we however simply called it the 'free crisps to the enemy effect'!'

[This example is provided with the kind assistance of Malcolm Follos of the Bowman Group.]

Example 13 - Making Measurement Real in the WUYJ Programme

At a national level, the potential benefits of the Wiring Up Youth Justice (WUYJ) Programme were reflected in the improvement targets set for the youth justice system. But how to make this contribution real at a local level? The programme worked with local management to ensure that change happened by making measurement meaningful and by 'keeping it real and keeping it simple'. This meant developing a suite of measures that were meaningful to the users (those who do the change), managers/decision makers (those that make the change happen) and stakeholders (those that fund or have an interest in the change).

Engaging local users was an area of particular focus. Getting local management to agree to cashable benefits can be both problematic and counter-productive – it turns people off the system and so damages the exploitation of capability that creates value. This is particularly so in a cross agency environment such as the youth justice system. The WUYJ programme recognised this by focusing on articulating and agreeing a set of behaviours that have been shown to produce better outcomes for young people. In this way, the measurement process becomes a catalyst for change. Active measurement was also recognised as bringing important by-products in terms of evidencing early gains and so addressing the, 'what's in it for me?' question.

The value of this approach was recognised in an independent review which concluded, "*The process for identifying, agreeing and managing the intended benefits is to be commended. Such an end user focused and inclusive approach means that tangible benefits are being realised and appreciated by the YOTS and wider YJS.*"

[Provided with the kind agreement of Phil Sutton, WUYJ – Head of Business Change and Benefits and Lisa Stewart, WUYJ Benefits Manager.]

This leads us nicely to the penultimate chapter where our focus is on how we can combine everything we have covered to date in moving beyond benefits realisation to creating additional value from our investments in ICT and IT enabled business change.

Chapter 9
Creating Value from ICT

"Nothing can have value without being an object of utility"

Karl Marx

Introduction

So far we have focused our attention on ensuring that firstly, benefits forecasts are robust and realisable, and secondly, that we identify all forms of potential value. We then considered how we can track these benefits from planning through to realisation. These are all integral steps to creating and managing value from our investment in ICT, but we can and should go further because:

- firstly, our philosophy in benefits planning has if anything been to tend towards the pessimistic to counter the usual tendency towards optimism in benefits forecasting. On the one hand this means that we can have some confidence that the benefits used to justify an investment can and will be realised. On the other, it means with the appropriate tools and techniques, benefits realised can, and indeed should, exceed those that were planned – whilst we are pessimistic in planning, we should be optimistic in exploiting the value created. This is not a contradiction – as Lovallo and Kahneman (2003) argue, "*draw a clear distinction between those functions and positions that involve or support decision making and those that promote or guide action. The former should be imbued with a realistic outlook, while the latter will often benefit from a sense of optimism.*"

- secondly, as we said in the Introduction to this section, things change and we need to ensure our focus is on creating value by realising benefits in today's conditions, rather than tracking an out of date set of assumed benefits; and

- thirdly, the reality is that in many cases benefits are emergent i.e. they evolve as we combine technology, process and people changes. We therefore need to ensure that our approaches to benefits management are sufficiently flexible and adapt to learnings on how ICT can be exploited in practice.

What we too often see in practice are situations where benefits management is backward-looking and focused on holding people to account for benefits as originally forecast, but which are now out of date. As a consequence, people's attention shifts to appearance manipulation and assigning the blame for non-realisation of benefits – and if people's attention is on defending themselves it can't be on creating value.

Donald Marchand (2006) at IMD argues that the IT project management paradigm, with its focus on deployment on time and to budget and key success factors of "*accessible*" and "*available*", is, "*deeply flawed and incomplete*". The problem is that the process of investing, managing delivery and realising benefits are seen as three distinct phases with limited overlap. Thus the business case is used as a means to obtain funding and then is forgotten only to be revised when an external review is scheduled. Once the business case has served its purpose in gaining funding, attention shifts to development and implementation of the IT with some limited user engagement near the end of this phase focused on system familiarity training. In the final phase, the project team has disbanded and responsibility for, and the additional work associated with, benefits realisation is handed over to the business.

In this chapter, we argue for a fundamentally different approach – one that has a forward-looking perspective, that manages benefits from an enterprise perspective as well as a project basis, and which is based on a process of continuous participative engagement between the IT function and business users throughout the project life cycle, which itself extends beyond roll out to benefits realisation. This process of continuous engagement encompasses the use of stories that engage the user in a joint exploration of, 'what might be'. Jaworski (1998), for example, explains how Shell's scenario planning process is, "*not about making plans, but is the process whereby management teams change their mental models of the business environment and the world...scenario planning is a trigger to institutional learning*" and a means to, "*create and discover an unfolding future.*"

Enterprise benefits management

The problem with managing benefits from a project perspective are that: usually the benefits won't be realised until after the project team has disbanded; projects don't realise benefits, the business does; we risk ignoring benefits from cross-departmental initiatives; and the reality is that too often insufficient attention is given in the business case to how benefits will be realised. In particular, the costs of the business change upon which benefits realisation is dependent are often excluded from the business case for the ICT 'solution'. The result is that anticipated benefits aren't realised and potential value is lost. The solution is to plan and manage benefits from an organisational or enterprise rather than a project basis and this requires that:

1. Project benefits realisation plans are summarised into a benefits realisation plan for the organisation for the year ahead.

2. This plan is reviewed to ensure that all benefits are captured – including those from projects funded by other organizations.

3. The annual benefits realisation plan is then reviewed by senior management who focus on the fundamental question – "*in the context of our investment to date and the environment in which we are now operating, is this the best that we can do?*"

4. Regular reports on progress are made throughout the year – focusing on both realisation of benefits against plan, as well as the effectiveness of the process and whether anything else can be done to enable greater value creation.

Managing benefits from an organisational or enterprise perspective also means that we can track the 1/10th of a person type savings – whilst it may be difficult to realise five minutes here and five minutes there, if we have several projects all delivering time savings we should, over time, be able to realise at least some of these savings.

Experience shows that managing benefits from an enterprise perspective is facilitated by the establishment of a Value Management Office (VMO). This does not necessarily imply setting up another central monitoring body – the role can fall to an existing function (such as the PPM Centre of Excellence) or it can be a virtual function encompassing activities undertaken by various other groups. But what a VMO provides is a function that provides oversight of the benefits management process and in particular a focus on value creation that includes:

- Helping to validate benefits forecasts and ensure that they are robust and realisable by:

    o Maintaining and updating the organisation's Benefits Eligibility Framework and developing a standard set of templates to streamline business case preparation.
    o Providing a robust and independent challenge to the assumptions that underpin benefits forecasts and asking are they reasonable.
    o Checking benefits forecasts for double counting.

- o Helping business case writers and business sponsors to prepare business cases that are consistent with the organisation's Benefits Eligibility Framework and which provide a clear line of sight from investment objective through to benefits realisation. The objective is to design robust business cases into the process rather than to inspect out dodgy cases.
  - o Tracking project performance in terms of benefits realisation compared with forecast over time and using this data to inform future forecasts.

- Ensuring all potential benefits are captured:

  - o Facilitating benefits workshops and completing benefits maps.
  - o Maintaining the high level organisational Strategy Map (Vision, Strategies and Measures) against which projects can map their strategic contribution via benefits mapping.
  - o Training IT and project team members in benefits modelling.
  - o In the public sector, sponsoring research into social value.
  - o Ensuring all sources of value are articulated, quantified and, where appropriate, valued. This helps overcome the issue where a project team has identified sufficient benefits to pass the organisation's hurdle rate for investment and sees no value in working to identify more. In such circumstances, the VMO can challenge the team to identify and quantify additional value that would otherwise have been ignored. The question that should be asked of all business cases is not just whether sufficient benefits have been identified to justify the investment but also whether any other benefits are possible.

- Facilitating benefits realisation and value creation:

  - o Compiling the enterprise-level Benefits Realisation Plan.
  - o Tracking the accumulated investment in ICT and the actual and forecast benefits from this investment. Sunk costs are not forgotten – rather there is transparency of the investment made as an incentive to seek additional benefits.

- Maintaining visibility of efficiency savings i.e. all those parts of a person saved, and to highlight where the combined position implies that staff can be re-deployed to activities elsewhere.
- Compiling benefit progress reports, and also analysing them and alerting management to areas where action is required – both in terms of bringing realisation back onto track and in terms of leveraging learnings to realise additional benefits.
- Monitoring and evaluating the effectiveness of the benefits management activity overall – and developing proposals for its enhancement.

Other key roles include undertaking post implementation reviews and educating and coaching business users in applying active benefits management. Lin et al (2005) for example, cite a VMO being established in an Australian public sector organisation to educate users about the benefits realisation process and to minimize resistance to its implementation.

The role is consequently an active one that combines robust scrutiny with a pro-active search for value. If it's to fulfill these roles effectively, the VMO needs to be independent of any project or programme delivery responsibility (to demonstrate its objectivity) and to have access to the requisite skills in benefits analysis, ICT project management and business awareness, to ensure that its appraisals and evaluations are credible. VMO staff also need to be brave and, as we suggested in Chapter 1, *"wise enough to play the fool."*

Fundamental to making this approach work is a culture of planning for success rather than attributing blame where the emphasis is on learning rather than identifying failure. Yes hold people to account, but the accountability works both ways and is a joint accountability between funders, project team and the business recipient of the system. Leadership is crucial in this regard – in clearly communicating expected standards of behaviour and in shifting the default mode of thinking from tracking against plan and justifying variances, to exceeding plan and creating value. This in turn requires that the reward and recognition processes are aligned with value creation and that benefits managers spend less time, 'linked by umbilical cord' to their computer screens, and instead actively engage with the users to identify and disseminate learnings about benefits realisation. As John Le Carré says, "*A desk is a dangerous place from which to view the world."* These issues of leadership, in demonstrating a commitment to new processes and behaviours, and user engagement, run through the remainder of our discussion.

Engaging Hearts and Minds - narrative leadership and the power of stories and storytelling

"Ideas come and go, stories stay"
Nassim Nicholas Taleb

"Why storytelling? Nothing else worked. Charts left listeners be-mused. Prose remained unread. Dialogue was just too laborious and slow."
Stephen Denning

Donald Marchand, Professor of Strategy Execution and Information Man-agement at IMD, argues that 75% to 80% of the value of ICT derives from usage rather than deployment (2006) and yet organisations typi-cally direct little effort at realising the value derived from increased usage of information and IT internally, by managers and staff, and externally, by customers/clients and suppliers (2004). Addressing this calls for an 'Information Orientation' (2001) which is people-centric and based on how people use and behave with information in the context of organisa-tional values – and this extends way beyond user training. We can argue about the exact percentage of value that is derived from usage, but the point is well made.

The other issue we need to bear in mind is that the sources of potential value will emerge over time as people realise how they can combine in-formation with other resources at their disposal (or potentially at their disposal if other business changes can be enacted) to improve services and deliver efficiency improvements. If we wish to get the most value from our investment in ICT we therefore need to engage users in an on-going dialogue and exploration about how to design and use the systems and information provided. But, as Benko and McFarlan (2003) argue, real breakthroughs take longer than expected because people walk, *"into the future backward, viewing the future through the lens of their past experi-ences."* Consequently, if we are to optimise our return on investment we need to change this lens to one that explores the future through a con-sideration of what might be and to engage users at an emotional level by tapping into their reserves of energy and enthusiasm. One way in which this can be achieved is via the medium of stories and storytelling which engage users, the project team and the IT function in a mutual explora-tion of the potential for change and how to create value from ICT. In this regard we can identify two types of story:

- Firstly, those that provide a stimulus to action by highlighting the risks we face by not changing (these were also discussed in Chapter 6); and
- Secondly, those that engage the audience in defining how ICT can be exploited to create a better future by painting a picture of what might be possible.

The former relate to 'Things Gone Wrong' whilst the latter seek to focus on the potential for 'Things Gone Right'. These two types of story are illustrated by two examples drawn from the United States and illustrate the effects of inadequacies in information sharing in the criminal justice context. The first, from Geerken (2002), highlights the unintended consequences that can occur when things do not go as intended and this provides a stimulus to calls for more effective sharing of information.

Example 14 - A call to action: 'Things Gone Wrong'

"On February 14, 2000, Kim L. Davis surrendered to the Independence, Missouri Police Department on a municipal warrant for possession for drug paraphernalia. He pled not guilty and bond was set at $1,000. Because he could not post the bond, he was transported to the Carroll County jail under a contract that jail has with the police department to hold some of its prisoners. On February 16, a warrant for probation violation was issued for Davis on an unrelated matter. On February 22, Davis changed his plea to guilty. A judge accepted his plea, gave him thirty days to pay the $150 fine, and ordered him released. Independence police faxed a release form to the Carroll County jail.

Independence police had checked Davis for warrants when he was booked on the 14th, but neither they nor Carroll County checked him for warrants on the 22nd, and he was released on 11:30am that day. Davis hitched a ride with an Independence police official, who dropped him in Independence. Christy Robel drove up to a restaurant with her 6-year old son Jake about a half mile from Davis's drop-off point. She left the keys in the ignition of her Chevy Blazer and went inside to get her son a coke, leaving him in the car. While she was inside, Davis jumped into the car and started to drive off. The mother chased the car and attempted to yank her son from the back seat as it was moving, but the boy got twisted in the seat belt and was killed as the vehicle sped away and he was dragged to death. Several motorists apprehended Davis.

Newspaper reports indicated that Carroll County officials assumed Independence police had checked for warrants before release and Independence police said at the time that they made the same assumption about

---

Carroll County. Bill Pross, Public Information Officer for the Independence Police Department, told our interview that the only Independence police officer who could accurately check warrant systems was fired just a few days before Davis's release."

This form of 'story' helps provide a stimulus for change by demonstrating the implications of not acting. The problem, is that on their own, these are rarely enough – the stimulus to change can be strong, particularly where the 'story' captures the common mood or when the consequences are extreme, but the effect is often short lived with the motivating effect rapidly 'petering' out. This can be seen in instances of initiative fatigue where stakeholders understand the rationale for change at an intellectual level, but the impetus provided by the stimulus to avoid failure has lost emotional impact. People haven't forgotten the original message, it's just that it has lost much of its initial power to effectively influence action.

The use of such, 'Things Gone Wrong' stories therefore need to be reinforced by stories of the second type that engage stakeholders in a dialogue about what might be possible or what Denning (2001) terms, "*the common exploration of what might be*". This type of story is illustrated by the following example from Cresswell at al (2000).

Example 15 - The stimulus to action: 'Things Gone Right'

"*This was not what Detective Madrill had expected to be involved with when she joined the department five years ago. Lawrenceburg had not experienced a drug killing before. She could not draw on departmental experience. Recalling recent training on fighting drugs she had received through the Integrated Law Enforcement Distance Learning Network, she logs on to the Integrated Law Enforcement Intranet and conducts a search of the unsolved crimes MO (modus operandi) database using the unique features of the crime as search terms. She gets three hits - Evansville, Jeffersonville, and Seymour. Each hit has the name of the investigating officer with phone numbers. Then Detective Madrill searches the Indiana State Police home page looking for background and investigational tips on drug-related homicides. She downloads a five-page guide and notes that there are three references with phone numbers for additional assistance - First Sgt. Jim Lloyd, squad leader for the Indiana State Police homicide squad of the recently formed Bureau of Criminal Investigations, Lt. Chris Battison, Indianapolis Police Department Metro Homicide Task Force, and Special Agent Donna Fleetman, FBI. Detective Madrill reviews the Indiana State Police guide, reexamines the evidence in light of what the guide says, and makes notes on what further information she needs to obtain. She then contacts the officers in Evansville and Jeffersonville and First Sgt. Lloyd on the interactive video network from a room at the Lawrenceburg campus of Ivy Tech. She shows them pictures of the crime scene using the separate digital camera, which permits zooming in on different sections of the picture and discusses the crime. All four concur that this crime appears to fit in with the pattern seen at the other two cities and formulate a coordinated plan for tracking down the perpetrators. This includes setting up a public folder for each of them to put in information as well as posting to the Integrated Law Enforcement Council's drug and homicide bulletin board their information with a request for other agencies with similar crimes or tips to contact them. Now, every law enforcement agency in Indiana has been enlisted to help solve Lawrenceburg's homicide."*

So far so good, but in engaging the user in an exploration of how we can exploit our investment in ICT to create value we can go further by:

- Making the story more memorable by using verbal presentations as well as the written word, so engaging the audience's attention by both sight and hearing;
- Making the story 'live' by incorporating a physical component;
- Enabling the story to adapt as the programme progresses; and
- Enhancing audience engagement by actively involving stake-holders in the story.

These aspects are illustrated by the example of the 'Criminal Justice Experience'.

Example 16 – The Criminal Justice Experience: exploring the 'imagine if'

The 'Criminal Justice Experience' was a one hour virtual walkthrough of the Criminal Justice System designed to support the CJS IT portfolio by showcasing the end-to-end process, the changes achieved to date and how ICT projects and programmes could make a difference to the efficiency and effectiveness of the criminal justice system and impact on front line staff, victims and witnesses. The objectives of the 'Experience' were defined as follows, to:

- give information in an engaging, modern and believable way;
- provide a fun/engaging environment to encourage understanding and participation;
- address public misconceptions about the criminal justice system and increase public confidence so it was seen to be effective;

- encourage the public to participate in the delivery of justice; and
- help reposition the Criminal Justice *System* as a *Service*.

It was targeted at a range of stakeholders including:

- sponsors (Her Majesty's Treasury, Cabinet Office etc);
- delivery partners (criminal justice organisations including the Police, Crown Prosecution Service, Courts, Prisons, Probation Service and Youth Justice officials – at national and local level);
- regulators such as the Office of Government Commerce, the National Audit Office and Prime Minister's Delivery Unit; and
- opinion formers (Media, Think tanks etc).

The 'Experience' commenced with participants watching a short video of a crime. They were then invited to participate by playing the role of key characters – the criminals, the victim and a witness. Participants then physically walked through the system visiting mock points/stages – arrest and charging with the Police; building the case with the Crown Prosecution Service; an initial hearing at the Magistrates' court; the full hearing at the Crown Court; the route of one offender through the Youth Offending Team; and the path of the second adult offender through Prison and Probation. At each stage the audience received an overview of the processes, the effect on the 'players' (the criminals, the victim and the witness) and the potential of the IT programme to make the system more efficient and effective. This was reinforced by the use of visual display boards and presentation material illustrating the process and key benefits. These overviews were presented by trained members of staff acting as narrators at each stage. The 'Criminal Justice Experience' ended with a feedback session where visitors were invited to ask more detailed questions and discuss any issues and thoughts the 'walkthrough' had stimulated.

More than 1,500 stakeholders including ministers, the media, staff from criminal justice and other organisations, as well as international criminal justice bodies, participated in the tour with satisfaction ratings of over 90%. Participants were provided with a printed version of the 'Experience' which was also available online.

The 'Experience' was found to deliver a number of key benefits:

- it helped raise the profile of the scope of the programme with key stakeholders;
- it facilitated a meaningful, on-going dialogue between business representatives and the IT programme;

118

- it was a very effective way of engaging key stakeholders and providing an end-to-end view of the system;
- being held on a fortnightly basis meant that presenters had to stay up to date with progress;
- it provided a basis for further development and expansion to encompass the wider business reform programme; and
- it provided the setting and context for using stories at each stage that could themselves change and evolve over time – these included the following example used to illustrate the power of information sharing via the Crown Prosecution Service's Case Management System (CMS).

Case Study: CMS in action

"*When a lorry fire on a motorway prevented a CPS file being delivered to the prosecuting lawyer at the Crown Court it looked like a potentially dangerous criminal could go free on bail. The defence counsel made a bail application on the basis that the prosecution could not establish the grounds for opposing bail without any paperwork, therefore compelling the Judge to accept the defence version of events. However, they hadn't counted on the CMS! The case had initially been logged by a duty lawyer working at a charging centre. Details were sent electronically to the magistrates' court and the case was subsequently referred to the Crown Court, with details being updated on the CMS. The availability of a secure computer terminal at the Crown Court allowed the prosecutor opposing bail to call up the case details and the defence subsequently withdrew their application. The defendant was remanded in custody on charges of possession with intent to supply, grievous bodily harm, kidnap, and intent to kill. The defendant was subsequently convicted of having an offensive weapon, assault occasioning actual bodily harm, common assault and possessing a Class B drug – resulting in a sentence of three and a half years' imprisonment*".

[Sourced from:
http://www.eurim.org.uk/activities/pi/data sharing case studies/dscs9 l ogicacmg.pdf Last accessed 15.11.08].

Section 3. Summary

Managing benefits so that they are realised in practice is not a passive, backward looking, reporting against plan process. Instead it should be an active, forward-looking process, with a bias for action and:

1. Based on joint accountability for benefits realisation with responsibility shared between the project, IT function, users, and the funding bodies.

2. Rather than starting post-implementation, this process should run throughout the project life-cycle with regular reviews as part of the portfolio stage/phase gate process to re-confirm the benefits justification and culminating in a re-commitment to realisation by the recipients.

3. Booking benefits wherever possible in efficiency plans, headcount targets, unit budgets, organisational strategy and delivery plans, and individuals' performance objectives – so providing a clear line of sight from strategic intent through to benefits realisation.

4. Tracking and reporting benefits against forecast but with a view to exceeding forecast and learning how to exploit the capability and capacity created.

5. Moving beyond tracking forecast benefits to value creation by managing benefits from an enterprise perspective and continuous participative engagement between the IT function, project teams and system users in an exploration of what might be.

6. Continually asking, in the context of our accumulated investment in IT and IT-enabled business change, "*is that the best we can do?*"

Chapter 10
Conclusions

"I conceive that the great part of the miseries of mankind are brought upon them by false estimates they have made of the value of things."

Benjamin Franklin

We started out by asking whether, in the context of a continuing failure to realise benefits, demonstrating a return on investment in ICT projects is a fool's errand. We concluded that the answer is 'yes', although not in the sense that it can't or shouldn't be done. Rather, we need someone willing and able to challenge the assumptions that masquerade as facts in our business cases and a different approach to the way we manage benefits more generally – remembering that benefits management has three objectives:

1. to ensure that benefits claims are robust and realisable;
2. to capture all forms of value created; and
3. to realise benefits and create value.

Ultimately investment in ICT is neither good nor bad – what determines whether it's a good investment or not are two factors: firstly, the value created, which depends on the use to which the ICT is put, and secondly, the relationship between the value so created and the cost incurred to create that value. Too often ICT projects and programmes seem to be a no-brainer – until things go wrong, at which point it becomes all too clear that the problems could be traced back to the business case. Ultimately, optimising the return on ICT and demonstrating this return, requires estimates of costs and benefits that are robust and reliable. Unfortunately, empirical evidence and practical experience indicates that business case writers suffer from cognitive biases which lead them to be too optimistic in their estimates. Even worse, there is evidence that the way these business cases are developed means that they often suffer from 'strategic misrepresentation' and represent a form of benefits fraud – albeit a fraud that some stakeholders appear happy to accept. When we ask why we are unable to show the benefits from our investments, the answer is clear – to borrow from Bill Clinton's 1992 presidential campaign, "*it's the business case, stupid*". So the answer to realising a return from ICT needs to start with the Business Case and the Benefits Realisation Plan, including:

- More accurate demand estimating and benefits forecasting including adjusting estimates to reflect data from similar projects in the past (reference class forecasting);

- Independent scrutiny – by a 'fool', to challenge the assumptions that masquerade as facts;

- Triangulate forecasts using more than one value lens – going beyond financial metrics to use multi-criteria analysis;

- Where benefits are in the form of staff time savings, being clear that they are not a benefit but a voucher – and a voucher only has a value if it is used. The Benefits Realisation Plan should be clear about how time saved will be reallocated to other value adding activity;

- Agreeing benefits claimed with the recipients. It's a fundamental principle of benefits management that the value of a benefit is the value assigned to it by the recipient; and

- Above all, ensuring that we are clear about the benefits we are buying, when they will be realised and what measures and indicators will be used to evidence their realisation.

Once we have established some rigour and realism in our benefits forecasting, we also need to ensure that we capture all forms of value created and that means:

- Capturing efficiency benefits and booking them wherever possible in budget cuts, unit costs, headcount targets, efficiency plans etc;

- Using Strategic Contribution Analysis to understand the impact of ICT on key measures of strategic success – and booking these benefits via the strategic planning process;

- Capturing benefits that cross organisational boundaries along with benefits to citizens and wider social value;

- Recognising the value implicit in mandatory projects – by using a 'willingness to pay' approach supported by detailed analyses of forecast impact and confirmation that this impact could not be achieved more cost effectively; and

- Accounting for the flexibility or potential opportunity value inherent in infrastructure investments.

The third objective of Benefits Management concerns actually realising the benefits forecast and creating value by exploiting the capacity and capability created. This involves:

- Not getting diverted by analyses with hundreds of benefits. Apply the Pareto Principle or 80:20 rule – focus on the main benefits and if in doubt remember that end benefits should relate to the four primary investment objectives discussed in Chapter 1: to save money; to generate revenue; to contribute to a strategic priority; or because you have to maintain business as usual or meet a legal or regulatory requirement. The benefits process should identify the scale of contribution or impact under these four headings.

- Size is the enemy of understanding so use summary, 1 page reporting to identify and track benefits and maintain a clear line of sight from investment objective to benefits realisation.

- On-going accountability for benefits including regular recommitment to the realisation of the benefits via stage gate and portfolio level reviews.

- Managing benefits from an enterprise or organisational, rather than a project perspective, and as part of the wider change portfolio.

- Establishing a Value Management Office function to provide a continuing focus on benefits management beyond project closure and to take a pan-project portfolio perspective.

- Continuous participative engagement with the business and users – embedding the 'Voice of the Customer' in the design, development and deployment of ICT; using narrative leadership and story telling in a mutual exploration of how ICT can be used and exploited to add business value; and ensuring a formative approach to post implementation evaluation with a focus on learning.

- Having been pessimistic in our benefits forecasting, we should now be optimistic in implementation and exploitation – benefits realised should exceed forecast as we identify emergent benefits and exploit synergistic benefits on a portfolio basis.

Underpinning it all is an approach that focuses on value throughout the project life cycle and which sees ICT projects and programmes as investments and moreover, investments that require other people's money – either that of shareholders or taxpayers. So beyond the 'fool', we also need to be a steward – to ensure funds are invested and managed appropriately.

For those that wish to assess themselves against these standards, and the wider Active Value Management regime discussed throughout this book, I have included a short 20 question diagnostic maturity assessment as an Appendix to this chapter. It is intended that this be used to inform the development of a 'road map' to guide organisations to improved investment decisions and greater returns from their investment in IT-enabled business change. But as always, remember those rose tinted glasses - ask, '*is that the best we can do?*' and dare to employ a 'fool' to address those assumptions that masquerade as facts.

Appendix
Benefits Management Maturity Assessment

Key Benefits Management Principles	Strongly Disagree	Disagree	Agree	Strongly Agree
1. The organisation has adopted a comprehensive Benefits Eligibility Framework i.e. a set of rules and guidance on the classification, quantification, and valuation of benefits, that is used to facilitate level playing field investment appraisals, portfolio prioritisation, and to track benefits realised against forecast.				
2. Benefits claimed by each investment are supported by a clear cause and effect analysis (with supporting benefits maps, models, and dependency networks where relevant).				
3. Evidence-based forecasting is employed using past experience from similar projects (reference class forecasting) to inform benefits forecasts.				
4. The scale of benefits forecast is validated with the recipients wherever possible prior to investment.				
5. Effective independent benefits integrity checks are undertaken to challenge the assumptions underpinning each investment and to ensure all benefits claimed are robust and realisable.				
6. Each project or programme has a comprehensive Benefits Realisation Plan which in-				

Key Benefits Management Principles	Strongly Disagree	Disagree	Agree	Strongly Agree
cludes: any business changes on which benefits realisation is dependent; appropriate measures/indicators for all key benefits; how realisation will be tracked; who is responsible/accountable for benefits realisation; and the trajectory for benefits realisation.				
7. Where staff time savings are forecast, plans are in place for the realisation of this potential value by re-deploying the saved resources to other value-adding activities and the conversion ratio is reasonable.				
8. Business Cases and Benefits Realisation Plans reflect all potential benefits including: efficiency benefits (cashable and time savings); costs avoided; effectiveness benefits / performance improvements; social value in the public sector; reductions in risk; the foundation or potential opportunity value inherent in infrastructure investments; the value of regulatory/legal compliance and avoidance of 'things gone wrong'.				
9. In approving the Full Business Case, the Investment Board also explicitly approves the Benefits Realisation Plan.				
10. The benefits case is reviewed at regular intervals (project stage/phase gates and portfolio level reviews) and each review culminates in formal re-commitment to benefits realisation by the recipients.				

Key Benefits Management Principles	Strongly Disagree	Disagree	Agree	Strongly Agree
11. Benefits Management is accepted as a joint responsibility between the IT function, project teams and operational/business management.				
12. Wherever possible forecast benefits are booked in budgets, unit costs, headcount targets, efficiency plans, strategic targets and delivery plans.				
13. Benefits realisation is integrated into the organisation's performance management framework with accountability for benefits realisation clearly defined in individuals' personal objectives.				
14. Benefits measurement is integrated into the organisation's performance management framework with benefits measures being linked to the measures of strategic success (e.g. via Strategic Contribution Analysis showing the contribution of benefits to measures of strategic success).				
15. Benefits are tracked to ensure the 'performance matches the promise' and that where benefits fall behind trajectory effective action is taken to address the shortfall.				
16. Senior leadership actively and consistently demonstrate a commitment to value creation from the accumulated and planned investment in ICT.				
17. Benefits tracking and reporting are focused on exceeding				

Key Benefits Management Principles	Strongly Disagree	Disagree	Agree	Strongly Agree
forecast and learning how to exploit the capability and capacity created. New learnings are identified and disseminated rapidly. The organisation is 'hungry' for feedback on performance.				
18. Active continuous participative engagement with users throughout the project life cycle is utilised to identify and leverage potential benefits.				
19. Benefits realisation is managed on an organisational basis with regular reporting on benefits against plan at a portfolio level and regularly asking, "*is that the best we can do?*				
20. Post-implementation reviews are undertaken of completed investments to identify ways of increasing benefits realised and lessons learned are fed back into the benefits management process.				

Glossary

Benefit	An advantage, profit or gain attained by an individual or organisation. Benefits are usually realised in terms of: increased revenue or sales; cost and time efficiency savings; compliance with legal and regulatory requirements; maintenance of business as usual; contribution to a strategic target or business priority; and some capability or capacity that lays the foundation for the delivery of benefits from other projects and programmes.
Benefits eligibility framework	The set of rules about what benefits can and can't be claimed, how they should be quantified and valued. It provides: • a methodologically sound approach to measuring and valuing benefits realisation; • a consistent approach across the organisation's ICT portfolio providing a level playing field for appraising potential investments ex ante; and • a basis for measuring performance against forecast and evaluating project performance ex post.
Benefits 'fraud'	Instances where business cases are presented for funding where those making the case are at best negligent and at worst complicit in a form of deception – deception because they know the benefits presented to justify the investment are unlikely to ever be realised in sufficient scale to justify the investment of taxpayers' and shareholders' funds.
Benefits Integrity check	A series of validation checks to ensure benefits claimed are: • consistent with the organisation's Benefits Eligibility Framework; • adjusted for optimism bias; • consistent with initiatives elsewhere in the organisation's change portfolio; and • agreed with the recipients. The objective is to ensure all benefits claimed are robust and realisable.

Benefits management	Benefits management is a process that runs throughout the project life cycle – from investment justification and preparation of the business case, through project implementation, and beyond project closure to business as usual. It is a process that encompasses: benefits identification, articulation, quantification and valuation; validation; tracking and reporting; and harvesting or realising benefits. It has three main objectives. Firstly, it seeks to ensure that investment decisions are made on the basis of a robust and clear understanding of the potential benefits – in short, there should be no confusion about what benefits are being bought. Secondly, it aims to capture all potential forms of value created – to ensure our investment decisions are value led and to lay the basis for benefits realisation. Thirdly, it seeks to ensure that forecast benefits are realised in practice and that we go beyond realising forecast benefits to capture benefits as they emerge and create value by exploiting capability and capacity on an on-going basis.
Benefits mapping or modelling	Methodologies which graphically illustrate the cause and effect chain from initiative through to end benefits and investment objectives. They can be enhanced by including the enabling and business changes on which benefits realisation is dependent (benefits dependency networking) and by considering the degree of confidence in the logic chain.
Benefits profile	A single repository for the key information related to each material benefit – its classification (efficiency or effectiveness and cashable or non-cashable); the trajectory and scale of impact; any dependencies and assumptions; who is responsible for realising the benefit; the business changes required to realise the benefits; and the measures that will be used to track realisation.
Benefits realisation plan	A document that supports the full business case. It includes the benefits profiles and: • A summary of the key benefits and the trajectory (ramp up schedule) for their realisation; • Benefits maps to demonstrate the cause and

	effect chain underpinning benefits claims as well as assessments of confidence in each benefit being realised; ▪ Details of any process changes and impacts on staff (training, skills, competencies etc) on which realisation is dependent; ▪ Explicit details on how time savings will be realised; ▪ Governance arrangements including responsibility for business changes, realising benefits, reporting and addressing issues that arise, as well as arrangements for formal benefits reviews; and ▪ How the key benefits will be tracked and reported – including the data sources to be used, who will collect the data, how often and what measures and indicators will be used.
Business Case	A document which explores the rationale for investment and the options for achieving the desired business outcomes. Often prepared in the 5 case format promoted by the OGC – Strategic Case, Economic Case, Financial Case, Commercial Case and Project Management Case.
Cashable benefits	Financial benefits that include instances where: ▪ Current output is maintained but at lower input cost so that budgets can be reduced. ▪ Additional output or throughput is achieved but for the same input cost i.e. budgets are unaltered but unit costs fall. These benefits can be measured in terms of the increased throughput or output, or in financial terms i.e. the value of the reduction in unit costs. ▪ Improving the quality of current activity with consequent savings elsewhere in the system. ▪ Increased productivity that enables savings to be achieved elsewhere – for example, staff time savings can allow staff to take on extra tasks that would otherwise have required the recruitment of additional staff. The crucial point here is that additional staff would otherwise have been recruited – if not, the benefit is an opportunity value, see below. As in the second

	category above, these benefits can be measured in terms of the additional activity undertaken or in financial terms, as the costs avoided from not having to employ new staff.
Continuous participative engagement	The process of continuous engagement between the IT function, the project team and the users in confirming requirements, determining the most appropriate solution and identifying business benefits in the context of changing priorities and system learnings.
Cost avoidance benefits	Costs avoided include: the running costs of existing legacy systems replaced by a new system; improved service reliability resulting in less system outages or downtime; uncertain future costs associated with the failure of legacy systems; and the benefits of choosing one project option over another in achieving a given policy objective. Such benefits should be considered as part of the options appraisal but whether they are included in the benefits management regime will depend on whether they are relevant once the preferred option has been selected.
Cost-benefit analysis	Defined by the HM Treasury Green Book as, *"Analysis which quantifies in monetary terms as many of the costs and benefits of a proposal as feasible, including items for which the market does not provide a satisfactory measure of economic value."*
Cost-effectiveness analysis	Defined by the HM Treasury Green Book as, *"Analysis that compares the costs of alternative ways of producing the same or similar outputs."* The guidance 'Measuring the Expected Benefits of e-Government' (August 2003) further advises that, *"At a minimum, a thorough business case should prove that the preferred approach is the most cost effective way of delivering against target".*
Cross-organisational pro-	*"A programme requiring the committed involvement of more than one organisation to achieve the*

gramme	desired outcomes. Also referred to as 'cross-cutting' programmes." Source: Source – OGC 'Managing Successful Programmes'.
Customer proposition	A statement which clearly describes the user needs and how the initiative will meet them i.e. in short, a clear articulation of the user perceived benefits.
Direct benefits	Those benefits that are realised directly as a result of a project or programme and do not depend on other business change.
Disbenefits	Defined by the OGC as, "*the negative impacts of change"*. These can be treated by offsetting the benefits case or as additional costs.
Double counting	Where the same benefits are claimed by, and used to justify, more than one project or programme.
Economic benefits	Benefits expressed in monetary value that include both financial benefits and the value attributed to system performance improvements, outputs and outcomes.
Effectiveness benefits	The economic or monetary value attributed to system performance improvements, outputs and outcomes.
Efficiency Benefits	Staff time, equipment and other cost savings. These benefits are realised in: reductions in operating budgets; increased output for the same input cost (with consequently lower unit costs); and in time savings which can be re-deployed to other value-adding activities or which enable existing activities to be completed to a higher standard of quality. Efficiency benefits need to be checked to ensure that they are actually realised in practice i.e. that budget cuts and re-deployed staff are not achieved at the expense of output quantity or service quality.
EGAP-principle	The terms adopted by the World Bank to refer to the assumption in project forecasting that '*Every-*

	thing-Goes-According-to-Plan.
Emergent benefits	Benefits that emerge during the design, development, deployment and use of ICT rather than being identified at the very start of the project or programme.
Enabled benefits	Projects that provide capability that can be combined with other business changes that facilitate the realisation of benefits. The majority of ICT benefits are enabled i.e. they are only realised when the investment in technology is combined with business process re-engineering and people change (including training and re-deploying staff).
Enterprise benefits management (see also Recipient-based benefits management)	Whereby the focus of benefits management activity is on the benefits to be realised by the organisation in the next planning period from the accumulated investment in ICT.
Exceptions reporting	Highlighting variances beyond pre-set control limits for management action.
Financial benefits	Those benefits with a direct monetary value in terms of costs saved and/or revenue generated.
Foundation value (See also Potential opportunity value)	The value implicit in infrastructure investments which enables expansion of current applications and investment in new applications that will deliver business benefits.
Formative evaluation	An ex post evaluation in which the focus is on learning to improve the performance of the system. It is essentially forward looking as opposed to summative evaluation which compares a system against what was originally planned.
Green book	The HM Treasury publication 'Appraisal and Evaluation in Central Government' which constitutes binding guidance for government departments and executive agencies.
IS/IT and ICT	Information Systems is a general term to describe the use of hardware and software to deliver infor-

	mation to business. Information Technology is a wide-ranging term to describe the use of computers and telecommunications. Information Communication Technology (ICT) has largely taken over from IT and gives more emphasis to the fact that computing in the 21st century is highly dependent on data communication. (Source: Remenyi, D., Bannister, F., and Money, A. (2007) *The Effective Measurement and Management of ICT Costs & Benefits,* Third edition, Elsevier, Oxford).
Intangible benefits	Benefits that are difficult to quantify and measure reliably such as improved staff morale and decision-making. In such cases proxy indicators of such benefits can be developed.
Internal Rate of Return (IRR)	"*The annual percentage return achieved by a project, at which the sum of the discounted cash inflows over the life of the project is equal to the sum of the discounted cash outflows.*" (Source: CIMA, Management Accounting Official Terminology, 2000 edition).
Investment appraisal	Ex ante analysis of a project or programme to determine whether investment is justified and to select the most appropriate option for meeting the identified business need.
Investment evaluation	Ex post analysis to determine whether forecast benefits have been received (summative evaluation) and how additional value can be created & how the benefits management process can be improved (formative evaluation).
Modular projects	Defined by the Cabinet Office (2000) 'Successful IT: Modernising Government in Action' as, "*a discrete part of an overall programme of work that offers some value to the organisation, even if the other parts of the programme are not completed.*"
Net Present Value (NPV)	The value of future net cash flows (outflows less inflows) discounted at the relevant cost of capital (3.5% in the UK public sector). Where the cash

	outflows exceed the inflows the result is the 'Net Present Cost' or NPC.
Multi-criteria analysis	The use of financial as well as other relevant criteria in investment appraisal. Multi-criteria analysis is used by both the US government's Value Measuring Methodology and the Australian Demand & Value Assessment Methodology.
Office of Government Commerce (OGC)	An independent office of HM Treasury, established to help Government deliver best value from its spending.
Opportunity value / non-cashable benefits	The value of staff time saved where there is no immediate saving in budgets, unit costs or costs avoided. Rather the staff time saved can be redeployed to activities that would otherwise not have been undertaken. The result <u>may</u> be an improvement in quality, outputs and outcomes.
Optimism bias	The HM Treasury Green Book says that, "*There is a demonstrated, systemic tendency for project appraisers to be overly optimistic. This is a worldwide phenomenon that affects both the private and public sectors...appraisers tend to overstate benefits.*"
Payback	The period of time before the cash inflows from an investment exceed the accumulated cash outflows. Can use discounted or undiscounted cash flows.
Portfolio (ICT Project Portfolio)	The collection of ICT projects and programmes planned and in flight at any one time.
Portfolio (ICT Portfolio)	The collection of ICT projects and programmes planned and in flight at any one time as well as the investment in current business as usual systems.
Portfolio prioritisation	The process by which the portfolio of ICT projects, programmes and initiatives are selected that represent an optimum return on the available investment funds. This return can be in terms of cost savings, increased revenue, strategic contribution, legal/regulatory compliance and supporting busi-

	ness as usual.
Potential opportunity value (See also Foundation value).	The potential value from expansion of current applications and investment in new applications that is enabled by investments in infrastructure.
Programme	A collection of projects and other activities that are managed in a coordinated manner in order to achieve some overall desired outcome and benefits realisation.
Project	Defined by the OGC's 'Managing Successful Programmes' as, "*A particular way of managing activities to deliver specific outputs over a specified period and within cost, quality and resource constraints.*"
Quantitative benefits	Benefits expressed in terms of a quantifiable improvement (in financial, percentage or other terms) for example, costs (£) or time saved (hours/minutes).
Qualitative benefits	Benefits of a subjective or intangible nature.
Recipient-based benefits management (See also Enterprise benefits management)	Managing benefits from the perspective of the recipient rather than a project. The focus is consequently on benefits from all projects and programmes that will be realised by that business unit or other recipient, and extends beyond the life time of any individual project.
Reference class forecasting	Where project estimates of cost, time and duration are derived from what actually occurred in a reference class of similar projects rather than being built up from an understanding of the specific project alone. Developed from the research undertaken by Kahneman and Tversky.
Senior responsible officer/owner	Defined by the OGC's 'Managing Successful Programmes' as the individual who is ultimately accountable for successful delivery, that is, the successful achievement of desired outcomes and realisation of expected benefits from a programme.

Social value	A statement of the benefits delivered to wider society from investment in ICT projects and programmes.
Strategic misrepresentation	A term coined by Bent Flyvbjerg to refer to the planned, systematic distortion or misstatement of the costs and benefits used to justify an investment. It is seen as a rational response to incentives in the investment appraisal process. Addressing it calls for a combination of: independent scrutiny and validation of proposals; reference class forecasting; aligning incentives with more accurate forecasting; and improved accountability from tracking performance.
Strategic contribution analysis	A technique for determining a project's strategic contribution by combining: • a Strategy Map – a description of the organisation Vision, the strategies used to attain that Vision and the measures used to assess achievement of the strategies; with • a Benefits Map/Model showing how ICT systems, and enabling and business changes, can be combined to realise benefits – and how these benefits contribute to the strategic measures identified above.
Strategy mapping	A visual representation from organisational vision (the 'where'), through the strategies (the 'how') to the measures (the 'what') used to assess success.
Tangible benefits	Those benefits which are relatively easy to quantify and measure.
Value	As distinguished from benefits which refer to the specific individual improvements arising from an investment in ICT. Value is a more generic and collective term comprising all benefits realised from an investment, forecast and emergent.
Value management	The active management process designed to optimise the return from the accumulated investment

	in ICT.
Value Management Office (VMO)	A unit established with the remit to ensure that the organisation optimises the return from its accumulated investment in ICT.

List of references

AGIMO (2004) *Demand and Value Assessment Methodology*, Available at: http://www.agimo.gov.au/__data/assets/pdf_file/0004/52438/DAM_and__VAM_Manual.pdf [Last accessed 1 December 2008].

Andresen, J., Baldwin, A., Betts, M., Carter, C., Hamilton, A., Stokes, E., and Thorp, T. (2000) 'A framework for measuring IT innovation benefits', in Lin, C., Pervan, G. and McDermid, D. (2005) 'IS/IT Investment Evaluation and Benefits Realization Issues in Australia', *Journal of Research and Practice in Information Technology,* Vol 37, No. 3, August 2005.

Ashby, W.R. (1956) *An Introduction to Cybernetics, First Edition*, Chapman and Hall, London, UK.

Ayres, I. (2007) Supercrunchers, Why Thinking-By-Numbers Is the New Way To Be Smart, Bantam, New York.

Benko, C. and McFarlan, F.W. (2003) *Connecting the Dots,* Harvard Business School Press, Boston, Massachusetts.

Bichard, M. (2004) *The Bichard Enquiry Report,* TSO, London, Available at: http://police.homeoffice.gov.uk/publications/operational-policing/bichard-inquiry-report?view=Binary [Last accessed 1 December 2008].

Booz Allen Hamilton (2002) *Building a Methodology for Measuring the Value of E-Services,* Available at: http://www.estrategy.gov/documents/measuring_finalreport.pdf [Last accessed 1 December 2008].

Bottoms, A.E. & Wiles, P. (1996) 'Understanding Crime Prevention in Late Modern Societies', in T Bennett (ed) *Preventing Crime and Disorder,* University of Cambridge Institute of Criminology, Cambridge Cropwood series 1996.

Bradley, G. (2006) *Benefits Realisation Management,* Gower, Hampshire.

British Broadcasting Corporation (2000) 'Dome falls far below targets'. Available at: http://news.bbc.co.uk/1/hi/uk/844969.stm [Last accessed 1 December 2008]

Buehler, R., Griffin, D., and Ross, M (1994) 'Exploring the "Planning Fallacy": Why People Underestimate Their Task Completion Times', *Journal of Personality and Social Psychology,* Vol 67, No. 3, 366-381.

Cabinet Office (2002) *Successful IT: Modernising Government in Action*, Available at: http://archive.cabinetoffice.gov.uk/e-envoy/reports-itprojects/$file/successful_it.pdf [Last accessed 15 November 2008].

Cabinet Office (2006) *Customer insight in public services – "A Primer",* Available at: http://www.cabinetoffice.gov.uk/media/cabinetoffice/corp/assets/pu

blications/delivery_council/pdf/cust_insight_primer061128.pdf [Last accessed 1 December 2008].

Cabinet Office (2008) *Customer Journey Mapping,* Available at: http://www.cabinetoffice.gov.uk/public_service_reform/delivery_cou ncil/cjm.aspx [Last accessed 1 December 2008].

Cabinet Office (2008) *Promoting Customer Satisfaction Guidance on improving the customer experience in Public Services,* Available at: http://www.cabinetoffice.gov.uk/media/cabinetoffice/corp/assets/pu blications/delivery_council/pdf/cust_sat_guidance1.pdf [Last accessed 15 November 2008].

Cialdini, R.B. (2007) *The Psychology of Influence*, Collins, New York.

CIO Council (2002) *Value Measuring Methodology – How-TO-Guide*, Available at: www.cio.gov/documents/ValueMeasuring_Methodology_HowToGuid e_Oct_2002.pdf [Last accessed 15 November 2008].

Cooper, R.G. & Edgett, S.J. (2007) *Generating Breakthrough New Product Ideas,* Product Development Institute Inc., Canada.

Cresswell, A., Burke, G.B., and Pardo, T.A. (2006) *Advancing Return on Investment Analysis for Government IT A Public Value Framework*, Center for Technology in Government, University of Albany, Available at: http://www.ctg.albany.edu/publications/reports/advancing_roi/advancing _roi.pdf [Last accessed 1 December 2008].

Cresswell, A., LaVigne, M., Simon, S., Dawes, S., Connelly, D., Nath, S., and Ruda, J. (2000) *And Justice for All: Designing Your Business Case for Integrating Justice Information*, Center for Technology in Government, University at Albany/SUNY, 2000, Available at: http://www.ctg.albany.edu/publications/guides/and_justice_for_all/a nd_justice_for_all.pdf [Last accessed 15.11.08].

Curley, M. (2004) Managing Information Technology for Business Value, Intel Press, Hillsboro.

Denning, S.D. (2001) The Springboard How Storytelling Ignites Action in Knowledge-Era Organisations, Butterworth-Heinemann, Boston.

Department of Treasury and Finance (2008) *Investment Management Standard*, Available at: www.dtf.vic.gov.au/investmentmanagement [Last accessed15 November2008].

Economist (1994) 'The price of imagining Arden', December 3rd, p.106.

eGovMoNet (2008) *Annex 1 - Description of Work*, April 2008, ICT-PSP/2007/1.

Farbey, B., Land, F., and Targett, D. (1999) 'The moving staircase Problems of appraisal and evaluation in a turbulent environment', *Information Technology & People*, Vol 12 No. 3 pp238-252.

Flyvbjerg, B., Mette, K., Skamris, H., and Søren, L. B. (2002) 'Underestimating Costs in Public Works Projects: Error or Lie?',

142

Journal of the American Planning Association, vol. 68, no. 3, pp. 279-295.

Flyvbjerg, B. in association with COWI (2004) *Procedures for Dealing with Optimism Bias in Transport Planning*, Available at: http://www.dft.gov.uk/pgr/regional/ltp/major/proceduresfordealingwithopti3687?page=1 [Last accessed 15 November 2008].

Flyvbjerg, B., Mette, K., Skamris, H., and Søren, L. B. (2005) 'How (In)accurate Are Demand Forecasts in Public Works Projects', *Journal of the American Planning Association*, vol. 71, no. 2, Spring 2005.

Foley, K. (2006) *Using the Value Measuring Methodology to Evaluate Government Initiatives*, Proceedings of the 2006 Crystal Ball User Conference, Available at: www.crystalball.com/cbuc/2006/papers/cbuc06-foley.pdf [Last accessed 15 November 2007].

Friedman, L.S. (1977) 'An interim evaluation of the Supported Work experiment', *Policy Analysis*, 3: 147-170.

Gartner (2004) *Get Real: The Future of IT infrastructure*, Gartner, Inc., Available at: http://www.gartner.com/resources/125200/125227/executive_summary_get_real_t_125227.pdf [Last accessed 15 November 2008].

Gartner (2005) Show Me the Money: Advanced Practices in Benefits Realisation, Gartner, Inc.

Geerken, M.R. (2002) *Consequences of Inadequately Integrated Justice Information Systems, A project report*, March 2002, Center for Society, Law and Justice, University of New Orleans. Available at: http://azcjc.gov/cjrip/pubs/AZICJISDocs/Consequencestudy.pdf [Last accessed 15 November 2008].

GSA (2003) *High Payoff in Electronic Government*, Intergovernmental Advisory Board Federation of Government Information Processing Councils, May, 2003, Available at: http://www.gsa.gov/gsa/cm_attachments/GSA_DOCUMENT/High%20Payoff_R2F-aQX_0Z5RDZ-i34K-pR.pdf [Last accessed 1 December 2008].

Hastie, R. and Dawes, R. M. (2001) Rational Choice in an Uncertain World: The Psychology of Judgment and Decision Making, Sage Publications, Thousand Oaks, CA.

HM Government (2007) *Service Transformation Agreement*, Available at: http://www.hm-treasury.gov.uk/d/pbr_csr07_service.pdf [Last accessed 1 December 2008].

HM Treasury (2005) *Managing risks to the public: appraisal guidance*, Available at: http://www.hm-treasury.gov.uk/d/Managing_risks_to_the_public.pdf [Last accessed 1 December 2008].

HM Treasury (2003) *Measuring the Expected Benefits of e-Government*, August 2003, Available at:
http://www.ogc.gov.uk/documents/HM_Treasury_-_Measuring_the_expected_benefits_of_e-government.pdf [Last accessed 1 December 2008].

HM Treasury (2003) The Green Book Appraisal and Evaluation in Central Government, TSO, London.

Jaworski, J. (1998) *Synchronicity The Inner Path of Leadership*, Berrett-Koehler Publishers, San Francisco.

Kahneman, D. (2002) *Maps of Bounded Rationality: A perspective on intuitive judgment and choice*, Prize lecture, December 8, 2002, Available at:
http://nobelprize.org/nobel_prizes/economics/laureates/2002/kahnemann-lecture.pdf [Last accessed 1 December 2008].

Kahneman, D. & Lovallo, D. (2003) 'Letters to the Editor, Delusions of Success', *Harvard Business Review*, December, 2003, p 122.

Kahneman, D. and Tversky, A. (1979) 'Prospect theory: An analysis of decisions under risk', *Econometrica*, 47, pp 313-327.

Kaplan, J. (2005) *Strategic IT Portfolio Management*, PRTM, Inc., United States.

Kearns, I. (2004) *Public Value and E-Government*, Institute for Public Policy Research, Available at:
http://www.ippr.org/publicationsandreports/publication.asp?id=478 [Last accessed 1 December 2008].

Kelly, G. and Muers, S. (2002) *Creating Public Value An analytical framework for public service reform*, Strategy Unit, Cabinet Office, Available at:
http://www.cabinetoffice.gov.uk/media/cabinetoffice/strategy/assets/public_value2.pdf[Last accessed December 2008].

KPMG (2005) *Global IT Project Management Survey*, Available at:
http://www.pmichapters-australia.org.au/canberra/documents/irmprm-global-it-pm-survey2005.pdf [Last accessed 1 December 2008].

Lerner, J. (2002) You Got Nothing Coming Notes from a Prison Fish, Doubleday, London.

Light, M., Rosser, B., Hayward, S. (2005) *Realizing the Benefits of Project and Portfolio Management*, Gartner, ID number GOO125673.

Lin, C., Pervan, G. and McDermid, D. (2005) 'IS/IT Investment Evaluation and Benefits Realization Issues in Australia', *Journal of Research and Practice in Information Technology*, Vol 37, No. 3, August 2005.

Lovallo, D. and Kahneman, D. (2003) 'Delusions of Success - How Optimism Undermines Executives' Decisions', *Harvard Business Review*, July 2003, pp 56-63.

Mackie, P.J., Wardman, M., Fowkes, A.S., Whelan, G., Nellthorp, J. and Bates, J. (2003) *Value of travel time savings in the UK: summary report*, Department for Transport, Available at: http://www.dft.gov.uk/pgr/economics/rdg/valueoftraveltimesavingsi nth3130?page=1 [Last accessed 1 December 2008].

Marchand, D.A., Kettinger, W.J. and Rollins J.D. (2001) *Information Orientation: The link to business performance*, Oxford University Press, Oxford.

Marchand, D.A. (2004) 'Extracting the Business Value of IT: It is Usage, not just Deployment that Counts!' *Capco Institute Journal of Financial Transformation*, Issue 11, August 2004, p.127.

Marchand, D.A. and Hykes, A. (2006) 'Designed to Fail: Why IT-Enabled Business Projects Underachieve', *Perspectives for Managers*, IMD, No. 138, October 2006.

Moore, M.H. (1995) *Creating Public Value: Strategic Management in Government*, Harvard University Press, Cambridge, MA.

Mornan, B. (2006) 'Benefits Realization: Government of Canada Experience, A presentation to the Organization for Economic Co-operation and Development', *E-Government Expert Meeting: Cost and Benefit Analysis*, Paris, France, 6 February 2006. Available at: www.tbs-sct.gc.ca/emf-cag/outcome-resultat/benefits-avantages/benefits-avantages-eng.ppt [Last accessed 1 December 2008].

Mott MacDonald (2002) *Review of Large Public Procurement in the UK*, Available at: http://www.hm-treasury.gov.uk/d/7(3).pdf [Last accessed 1 December 2008].

NECCC (2002) *ROI Lessons Learned for E-Commerce or E-Government Projects*, Exposure Draft, December 5, 2002, Presented at the NECCC Annual Conference, December 4-6, 2002, Available at: www.ec3.org/downloads/workgroups/2002/roi_paper.pdf [Last accessed 15 November 2008].

NECCC IT Governance Work Group (2005) *Technology Investment Selection and Protection: The Governance Challenge*, Available at: http://www.ec3.org/workgroups_papers_2005.php [Last accessed 15 November 2008].

NOIE (2003) *E-Government Benefits Study*, April 2003, Available at: http://www.agimo.gov.au/_data/assets/file/0012/16032/benefits.p df [Last accessed 1 December 2008].

Office for Government Commerce (2003), *Managing Successful Programmes*, TSO, London.

Office for Government Commerce (2005) *Managing Benefits: An Overview Version 1.0*, Available at: http://www.ogc.gov.uk/documents/ManagingBenefitsV101.pdf [Last accessed 1 December 2008].

Office for Government Commerce (2005) *DVLA Change Programme - Benefits Management OGC Case Study,* Available at: http://www.ogc.gov.uk/documents/CP0019_DVLA_Change_Program-Benefits_Management.pdf [Last accessed 15 November 2008].

Office for Government Commerce (2005) *Successful Delivery Toolkit,* OGC, London.

Organisation for Economic Co-operation and Development (2006) *E-Government Project, Benefits Realisation Management,* GOV/PGC/EGOV(2006)11/REV1, Available at: http://www.olis.oecd.org/olis/2006doc.nsf/LinkTo/NT00009102/$FILE/JT03224718.PDF [Last accessed 1 December 2008].

Other People's Money (1991) Film, Directed by Norman Jewison, Warner Bros Pictures, USA.

Peppard, J., Ward, J., and Daniel, E. (2006) *Managing the Realization of Business Benefits from IT Investments,* Submission to MIT Sloan Management Review.

Piattelli-Palmarini, M. (1994) *Inevitable Illusions,* John Wiley & Sons, Inc., New York.

Public Accounts Committee of the House of Commons (1999) *Improving the Delivery of Government IT Projects,* Available at: http://www.publications.parliament.uk/pa/cm199900/cmselect/cmpubacc/65/6502.htm[Last accessed 1 December 2008].

Remenyi, D., Bannister, F., & Money, A. (2007) The Effective Measurement and Management of ICT Costs and Benefits, Elsevier, Oxford.

RSO SPA and Luiss Management (2006) *eGEP Measurement Framework Final Version,* Available at: www.epractice.eu/document/3610 [Last accessed 1 December 2008].

Sanwal, A. (2007) *Optimizing Corporate Portfolio Management,* John Wiley, Hoboken, New Jersey.

Seddon, J. (2008) *Systems Thinking in the Public Sector,* Triarchy Press, Axminster.

Senge, P.M. (1999) *The 5th Discipline,* Random House, Australia.

Sohal, A.S. and Ng, L. (1998) 'The role and impact of information technology in Australian Business', in Lin, C., Pervan, G., & McDermid, D. (2005) 'IS/IT Investment Evaluation and Benefits Realization Issues in Australia', *Journal of Research and Practice in Information Technology,* Vol 37, No. 3, August 2005.

Taleb, N.N. (2004) *Fooled by Randomness,* Penguin, London.

Taleb, N.N. (2007) *The Black Swan,* Allen Lane, England

Tallon, P.P. and Kraemer, K.L. (2003) *Creating business value with information technology: challenges and solutions,* IGI Publishing, Hershey, PA.

Thorp, J. (2003) *The Information Paradox,* McGraw Hill, Canada.

University of California Berkeley (2006) *Flyvbjerg to present first wachs lecture: "Survival of the unfittest"*, Available at: http://www.its.berkeley.edu/news/wachslecture.1.html [Last accessed 1 December 2008].

Varney D (2006) A better service for citizens and businesses, *a better deal for the taxpayer*, HMSO, Norwich, Available at: http://www.hm-treasury.gov.uk/d/pbr06_varney_review.pdf [Last accessed 15 November 2008].

Wachs, M. (1989) 'When Planners Lie with Numbers', *APA Journal*, 476, Autumn.

Ward, J. (2006) Delivering Value from Information Systems and Technology Investments: Learning from success, Information Systems Research Centre, Cranfield.

Ward, J. and Daniel, E. (2006) *Benefits Management Delivering Value from IS/IT Investments*, John Wiley & Sons, Chichester.

Ward, J. and Taylor, P. (1996) 'Realising the Business Value of IT: Managing the Benefits', *Enterprise Analysis 7*, Cranfield School of Management.

Weill, P. and Aral, S. (2004) 'Managing the IT Portfolio: Returns From The Different IT Asset Classes', MIT Sloan Center for Information Systems Research, *Research Briefing*, Vol IV, Number 1A, March 2004.

Weill, P. and Johnson, A. (2005) 'Managing the IT Portfolio (Update Circa 2005): Where did the infrastructure go?', MIT Sloan Center for Information Systems Research, *Research Briefing*, Vol V, Number 3A, December 2005.

Wormeli, P. (2006) IT By the Numbers Performance Measures for information technology projects, IJIS Institute, United States.

Yu, O. (2008) 'Application of real options analysis to technology portfolio planning: a case study', *International Journal of Quality & Reliability Management*, Vol 25, No 1 pp 52-59.

Index